THE A B C OF POT PLANTS

THE ABC OF GARDENING SERIES

THE ABC OF GARDENING (Key Volume)
THE ABC OF BULBS AND CORMS
THE ABC OF CACTI AND SUCCULENTS
THE ABC OF CARNATIONS AND PINKS
THE ABC OF CLOCHE GARDENING
THE ABC OF DAHLIAS
THE ABC OF FLOWER GROWING
THE ABC OF FLOWERING SHRUBS
THE ABC OF FRUIT GROWING
THE ABC OF GARDEN PESTS AND DISEASES
THE ABC OF THE GREENHOUSE
THE ABC GUIDE TO GARDEN FLOWERS
THE ABC OF THE HERBACEOUS BORDER
THE ABC OF HERBS, SALADS AND TOMATOES
THE ABC OF POT PLANTS
THE ABC OF PRUNING
THE ABC OF THE ROCK GARDEN AND POOL
THE ABC OF ROSES
THE ABC OF SOILS (Including Manures, Composts and Lawns)
THE ABC OF VEGETABLE GARDENING

THE A.B.C. OF
POT PLANTS

W. E. SHEWELL-COOPER

M.B.E., N.D.H., F.L.S., F.R.S.L., DIP. HORT. (WYE), D.LITT.
Chévalier du Mérite Agricole (France)
Fellow of The Horticultural College (Vienna Univ.)
Director, The International Horticultural Advisory Bureau
Lately Command Horticultural Officer, S.E. and E. Commands
Sometime Horticultural Superintendent, Swanley Horticultural College
Horticultural Advisor, Warwickshire and Cheshire County Councils and
Garden Editor, B.B.C. North Regions.

THE ENGLISH UNIVERSITIES PRESS LTD
102 NEWGATE STREET
LONDON, E.C.1.

First printed in this form 1958
Second Impression 1963

Made and Printed in Great Britain for the English Universities Press, Ltd., London
by C. Tinling & Co. Ltd., Liverpool, London and Prescot.

CONTENTS

Dedicated to
My dear Friends
BASIL and the late MARGARETHA FURNEAUX

LIST OF COLOURED ILLUSTRATIONS

AUTHOR'S PREFACE

THERE is something very satisfactory about owning and growing a pot plant. Cut flowers are very beautiful indeed but, however carefully you keep them in water, they don't last much more than ten days. A well grown flowering pot plant, however, may go on giving pleasure for many months of the year, while many of the evergreen types last for years.

I don't think we are quite so pot-plant-minded in this country as they are on the Continent. I usually go over and see the horticulturalists of other countries at least twice a year and recently I spent a lot of time with the pot plant growers in the " environs " of Paris. The owner of one of the largest nurseries there told me that he knows from the number of pot plants he sells each season that every second family in the whole of that big city buys at least one pot plant a year. His sales figures are absolutely astronomical! It isn't that all the pot plants die each season. In many cases families start with one pot plant and then go on until they have twenty or more in different parts of the house.

I have a friend who has married a Swedish girl and she has taught me a lot about the use of pot plants. In Denmark and Norway too they have great skill in the growing of plants in the houses. During these last few years the interest in pot plant culture in Great Britain has been increasing. This is to a great extent because people are travelling more and a far greater representative proportion of folk in this country are spending their holidays on the Continent. They see pot plants being used there in large numbers and they think that they'd like to emulate the idea in their own homes.

There are of course thousands of families who have no gardens at all. They live in our towns and cities in flats, and so the only way in which they can take part in that fascinating hobby " gardening," is to grow plants indoors. There are just as many keen gardeners in flats as there are in the country.

It isn't the town dweller's fault that he has not got a fair acreage of land to cultivate; this is due to the exigencies of modern civilisation.

Curiously enough, however, it is by no means the town dweller who has the monopoly of the pot plant. Cottagers in the country often specialise in different types of plants grown in pots and you find their windows full of them. This is particularly true perhaps in the case of Geraniums.

Some people have conservatories, and here they grow pot plants by the dozen and it is wonderful what kaleidoscopic displays it is possible to have under these conditions. At the Horticultural Training College, Thaxted, for instance, there is a small, electrically-heated greenhouse that is kept bright with pot plants all the year round.

I have confined myself to the large number of pot plants that one can grow comparatively easily in this country. There is almost no end to plants that *can* be grown in pots. Friends of mine, for instance, have raised little oaks from acorns, little citrus trees from pips of oranges and lemons, and have even dug up little plants from the woodlands and hedges. However, I hope that within the confines of this book you will find all the pot plants that you will want to grow. There are certainly large numbers to choose from.

I am very thankful to Miss Mary Morris and Mrs. Gweneth Johnson both ex-staff of The Horticultural Training College, for reading through the proofs, and I must thank my secretary, Miss Brenda Harman also for typing all the script. Mr. M. W. Gibson was most helpful with all the lists of plants—as an old Head Student of the Horticultural Training College—he naturally took a great interest in the book.

W. E. SHEWELL-COOPER.

The International Horticultural Advisory Bureau,
Arkley, Herts.

CHAPTER 1

MAKING A CHOICE

It is indeed fortunate that those of us who love growing plants in pots have a great variety to choose from. I have been fascinated sometimes when travelling round the country to find cottagers—who have quite a big garden of their own—insisting on growing all kinds and types of plants indoors, and thus making their homes as beautiful as the gardens outside.

There are others who love to watch plants grow, and they like to start right from the beginning. They plant a pip of an apple, or orange, in suitable soil. Then they watch the little seedling come up and develop, first of all into a fascinating little plant, and later into quite a big tree. There is something peculiarly possessive about being able to say, "I raised that tree myself. I had it right from the beginning. It's all my own work." Actually, of course, it is God's work, but the person concerned was a worker together with Him in this particular instance. Something is said in fact about sowing seeds in Chapter 6.

Some people much prefer to have flowering plants. They don't care for the poor old Aspidistra. They think that this is dull. They therefore like to grow Cyclamen, or Primulas, or maybe Geraniums. They become quite adept at it, and when you go to see them they always have some pots in flower. It is curious the way that plants die with some people very quickly and live for long periods with others, isn't it? Actually of course the reason why plants die early is because they are not given the right treatment, and the whole point of this book is to tell you how to get the best results with the minimum of labour.

Then there are those who are perfectly satisfied with foliage plants. They love the green leaves. They get a great deal of pleasure from seeing the sunlight playing on the foliage. They are happy to transform a maybe rather uninteresting room into a regular bower, and remember that there are some very beautiful types of variegated foliage plants which take little or no growing at all. After all, if you have a room where the windows are overshadowed, then there may quite easily be more shade than sun. Flowering plants, therefore, wouldn't be suitable, but you could easily grow what people call a Castor Oil plant (*Fatsia japonica*), and there are variegated types to be had of this plant, though few know about them.

Many people lately have turned to the climbing plants, and personally I think that these are extremely fascinating. A friend of mine has married a Swedish girl and she had introduced into the house numbers of climbers which grow most beautifully up the walls and over the mantelpiece. She has them around the pictures, and one even climbing up the wrought iron lamp-standard. Many of them are Philodendrons and one of them with heart-shaped leaves is very hardy and very easy to grow.

Then there are those who prefer shrubs. Being an Australian, my wife is very fond of the Eucalyptus, which she of course calls the Blue Gum. If you get hold of a seedling early in the year, you will find that it grows like fury, and before Christmas you could easily have a tree touching the ceiling. The disadvantage of a quick growing shrub of this kind, of course, is that you have to keep on re-potting it, and that isn't always convenient in a flat or small house. There's another shrub that I love; most people call it the Genista. Actually its real name is *Cytisus fragrans*. It is very popular in Wales, where they love to have it in flower round about the Easter period.

We've said nothing so far about the hanging plants. They are most fascinating to grow. You grow them in their pots or bowls and it isn't long before they start to cascade over the sides, and they could easily grow longer and longer if you let them have their own way. Some people have called them "Waterfall" plants for this reason. They have fascinating names like Wandering Jew (*Tradescantia fluminensis*) or the Strawberry Geranium (*Saxifraga sarmentosa*). You can read more about them in Chapter 11. At least one of the trailers or " cascaders " is very tiny, and is often grown in quite small pots for this reason. It is usually called " Mind your own business " (*Helxine Soleirolii*), but a prettier name is Baby's Tears. Creeping Charley (*Pilea nummularifolia*) is another which grows in such a way that it completely covers the pot, hanging down and looking very beautiful indeed.

One mustn't forget the cacti and succulents. They are very interesting. On the whole they are not flowering plants, but some of them do produce the most lovely blooms, some remaining open for several days and others only lasting a few hours. The plants may be grown on the windowsill or even on the mantelpiece. They love plenty of light, however, so keep the windowpanes clean and be sure to keep out " smog " and fog mists. You can either grow the plants in pots or you can use them to plant up little gardens made in deep trays or large bowls.

The Chinese and Japanese are experts at producing perfect specimens of dwarfed trees in pots and they can produce a tree only twenty inches high, which is a perfect miniature of one of the great specimens seen in the forest. (Actually there is a British Miniature Tree Society.) It is really wonderful to be able to grow a Douglas Fir or Japanese Larch, or even a Norway Spruce, and have it growing at home for years and years.

You will thus see that there is plenty of choice and in most cases, the plants that have been mentioned are those which are perennial or permanent. In Chapter 13 the bulbs and corms are dealt with in detail and one can always have a grand display in the spring by planting Hyacinths, Daffodils, Crocuses and so on. There are also annuals that can be grown in pots; simple plants like Calendulas, Godetias, Dwarf Cornflowers and the like, but once again these only last a few months like the bulbs, and most people in these days of financial stringency like to concentrate on plants that are more permanent.

However, before leaving this Chapter and the question of choosing, something must be said about " fitting your choice " into the type of house or flat, or room even, in which you live.

The man who has his garden or allotment is always happy to blame the neighbour's cats—the rain—the birds—and in fact anything but himself. You, however, who are going to concentrate on growing pot plants indoors will have only yourself to blame if anything goes wrong. If you fail to water them, there will be trouble. If you over-water, the soil will be sodden. If the plants stand in a draught, they will suffer; if you put them too near the window and there's a serious frost, they may be killed.

The great thing is to try and give the plants the kind of conditions that they would normally have when they are growing out of doors. Take an interest, therefore, in the background of the plant you are growing. Does it come from the arid desert, or does it grow naturally in the steamy water of swamps. If you pay a fair price for a good plant and you propose to keep it for ten years or so, then it will repay you to get to know something about it, because if you treat it well, it will be happy, and its very contentment will add " something " to your home.

Fortunately, in most parts of England electricity has replaced gas, and so we haven't got to worry very much about the poisoning which the fumes of the old gas jets used to cause. Furthermore, we can grow better plants now than the Victorians could, because we've cut out the heavy curtains and the draperies over the piano and mantelpiece. Most of our rooms, too, are distempered or papered in light colours, and so there is far more reflected light (which the plants love) than there was in the days when wallpapers were red and dark green and were covered with huge " awkward-looking " patterns.

It is useful, however, to know that there are plants which actually hate too much light—for instance the Fittonias whose lens-like cells have a capacity for " drawing in " every bit of light there is. I only wish, however, that these Fittonias lasted far longer. They usually die because they loathe draughts and too often get too much sun. The African Violets don't really want sun and my American friends tell me that they are the most popular pot plant in the U.S.A. They will grow in any warm room, but if there is one thing they dislike, it is central heating, which tends to make the air too dry. To make them happy, keep the pot surrounded by moist peat.

If you have to live in a smoky town or city and the conditions of the room always seem to be stuffy, you try and keep the smog out by closing the windows; you have to be away at work during the day and so the room doesn't get ventilated as it should; in this case there is a lot to be said for a plant like *Monstera deliciosa.* It is usually called the Swiss Cheese plant, and is sometimes incorrectly sold by the nurserymen as the *Philodendron pertusum.* I always say it's a plant that will stand any amount of brutality. It produces masses of aerial roots outside the pots, and you can cut these off because they may appear hideous. If it grows too tall, you just cut it back and it goes on quite happily. By the way, its peculiar method of producing the whitish roots like claws hanging from the stem have caused it to be called by some people the "Crocodile palm," so you may find it under this name.

Surely, I have said enough to show you that, (1) there are plenty of plants to choose from and you have only to go on reading through the book to see what I mean, (2) it does pay before choosing a plant to make certain where you are going to grow it, and then you can, so to speak, make sure that you provide your newly-found friend with the conditions it really likes. Don't be put off by what other people say; just grow the plants you like and, if you like them and look after them, they will like you and grow for you. You can have an ivy or an oak, Sansevieria or a Eucalyptus, a Geranium or a Cobaea, the latter will be happy on the hottest of windowsills!

CHAPTER 2

POTS—THEIR TYPES AND SIZES

As we are writing about pot plants, it is necessary, to say something about the containers in which the precious plants are to be grown. For hundreds of years now the majority of pots have been made out of porous clay, baked in a kiln. The idea being, that the soil in which rooting could take place could be held together. The bottom of a flower pot was invariably made flat, so that it could stand level on the bench in the greenhouse, or on a table in the home. In order to make certain that all the excess water could easily drain away, a hole was provided at the base of the pot and generally speaking, the larger the container, the larger the hole.

In most cases, pots are made with a fairly thick rim at the top for the purpose of adding strength. Some of the rims are curved, while others are much squarer with the idea of making it easier for the gardener to get hold of. The baby pots like the " thimbles and thumbs " do not have any rims at all, for these are not necessary. Most manufacturers make the 60's and small 60's without rims also, while some do not bother to put rims even on the 54's.

The reason that pots are given these peculiar numbers is that they are always sold by bulk, in what is called a " caste." The manufacturer uses exactly the same amount of clay for each caste: thus, if he is required to produce 3-inch pots he can make 60 of them with that particular quantity of clay, and so these are known as 60's. If, on the other hand, he has to make 9 or 9½-inch pots, he can only make 16 with a similar quantity of clay and these, therefore, are called 16's. Amateurs find it difficult to understand why the 60's should be the small size and the 12's the large size, and when you come to the largest pot of all, which is 18 inches across the top, it is known as a 2.

The drawing below does give an idea as to the sizes of the pots and what range can be had. I must say in passing that not all pot manufacturers make their pots in exactly the same way or to exactly the same degree in size. For instance, the

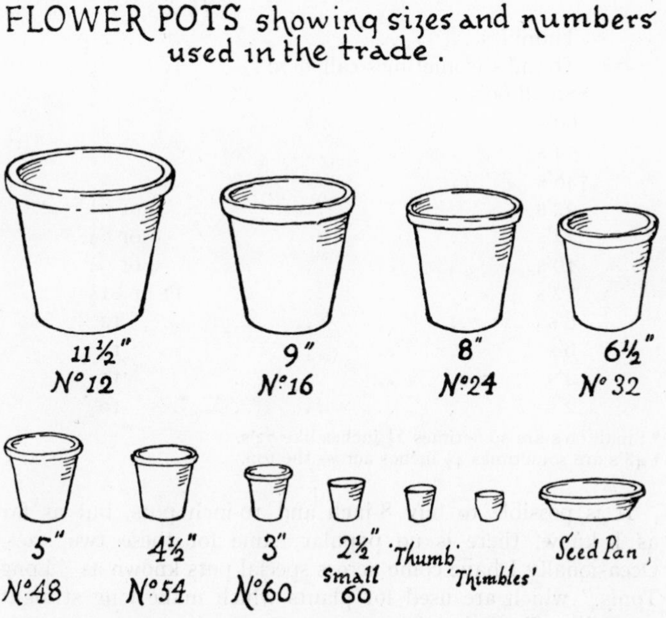

60's from firm A may be just a little bit larger than the 60's from firm B, but taking it all round they are about the same and gardeners have never grumbled. There are differences too in the actual nomenclature. For instance, most people think of 60's as being 3½ inches across the top and the same in depth, but very often now they are 3 inches deep and 3 inches across; 48's were normally 4½ inches across the top, but some sell a pot which is 5 inches across the top as a 48, and the pot that is 4½ inches across they call a 54.

It will be a good thing if some day the Royal Horticultural Society calls a conference of all pot makers so as to agree on a standard formula which can be used, not only right the way throughout the trade, but among all classes and types of gardeners also.

Pot sizes can then be said to be roughly as follows:

	Inches across the top
Thimbles	2
Thumbs (sometimes called 72's)	2½
*Small 60's	2¾
60's	3
54's	4½
†48's	5
32's	6 or 6½
24's	8 or 8½
16's	9 or 9½
12's	11 or 11½
8's	12
6's	13
4's	15
2's	18

* Small 60's are sometimes 2½ inches like 72's.
† 48's are sometimes 4½ inches across the top.

It is possible to buy 8-inch and 10-inch pots, but as far as I know, there is no popular name for these two sizes. Occasionally I have come across special pots known as "Long Toms," which are used for plants which make long straight roots, like Clematis. These pots are much deeper than the ordinary ones, as their name suggests.

Travelling about as I do, on advisory work, all over the country, it has been possible to meet with pot manufacturers who have deviated from the rules made above and have set out to make the pots stronger, so that though these may be only 3 inches across, they cannot get 60 out of a cast. Others have tried to get new sizes, and have produced square pots which they say fit easier into the staging of a greenhouse. It would be nice to have some trials carried out at the John Innes

Horticultural Institution on the whole question of pots and pot sizes, though I don't think any one really knows which is the best form of clay pot to use at the present time. All we do know is that under modern conditions the tendency is to use smaller pots and, whereas years ago we grew all our late Chrysanthemums in 12's, we try and do grow them today in 16's or even 24's, and get, surprisingly enough, very good results.

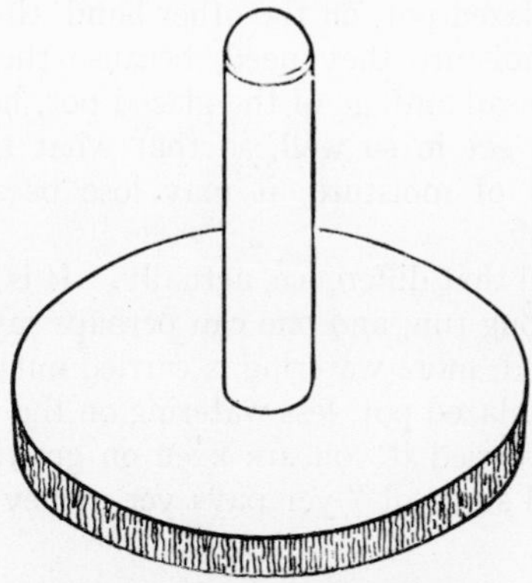

A round presser for pots, it presses the soil firm and level.

Porous Cement Pots

Some gardeners are very keen on using Porous cement pots rather than the ordinary clay ones. They claim that these pots last far longer and, being porous, are of just the same texture as the clay type pot. The Guernsey growers are particularly keen on them, and if you are visiting that Island, you will find hundreds of these porous cement pots in use in the greenhouses. At the moment, as far as I know, these pots are sold in four sizes only. A large 32, that is to say 6½ inches across the top and about 6½ inches deep; a small 16, or 9 inch size; a small 12 or 10 inch size, and the 8's or 12 inch size.

The Glazed Pot

Some shops now offer glazed pots in various colours. Some

of these have no drainage holes at all, while others are made in a similar manner to the clay pots. Such pots are more expensive, but for plants in the home they can be said to be definitely more attractive. It is claimed that these glazed containers help the plants, in that not so much moisture is lost through evaporation. The roots of plants, which always tend to circle round the inside of a clay pot, may easily be dried because the walls of the pot are constantly evaporating moisture. In the glazed pot, on the other hand, the roots seem to have all the moisture they need, because the sides are not porous. The disadvantage of the glazed pot, however, is that the air doesn't get in so well, so that what the plant gains through plenty of moisture, it may lose because it cannot breathe properly.

There isn't all that difference, actually. It is just a question of care in the long run, and one can perhaps say that if a clay pot is being used, more watering is carried out; and if a plant is growing in a glazed pot, less watering on the whole. Don't, therefore, be worried if you are keen on growing pot plants. It's the old, old story of " yer pays yer money and yer takes yer choice."!

Glass Pots

In some London stores one or two sizes of glass pots are offered. Most of these are of a brown or dark green colour, and they are quite attractive. One of the advantages is that you can actually see the roots growing and it is fairly easy to discover when the plants really need potting on. The author has not grown large numbers of plants in glass containers and so has very little to say about them, except that they are probably similar in effect to the glazed pots.

Plastic Pots

Latterly at the Horticultural Training College, Thaxted, we have been using large numbers of plastic pots, the reason being that these are almost unbreakable and, when teaching students, an unbreakable pot is a great advantage! We use 9-inch pots almost exclusively for growing Chrysanthemums and they appear to be very satisfactory indeed. At the moment they can be bought in most of the standard sizes. Actually, these pots are about the same price as the ordinary clay type, but the makers claim, naturally, that the great advantage is that they last longer, and so are a cheaper " buy " in the long run.

If there are any disadvantages to these plastic pots, these are probably that they don't dry out so quickly, because they are not porous, and there is tendency, therefore, for one to over-water. This is particularly true in the case of slow-rooting plants and when the loam in the compost is a little bit on the heavy side. We notice it particularly at the College when inexperienced students do the watering; a man can much more quickly over-water a plant in a plastic pot than in a clay pot.

On the other hand with the new plastic pots there is much less watering needed and that saves time. A 3-inch clay pot may need watering every day, but a plant in a plastic pot every 3 or 4 days only. Plastic pots also take up much less room and are far lighter.

Cardboard Pots

Though it is true to say that one cannot permanently grow plants in a house in pots made of cardboard, fibre, whalehide and the like, yet it may be worth while mentioning the fact that it is possible to buy such pots fairly cheaply, for the purpose of raising seedlings, or striking cuttings. Then, once the plants are well grown, they may be potted up into their clay or plastic pots with no root disturbance or check at all, for in the majority of cases pot and plant go in complete and the pot quickly rots in its new situation, and the roots go free.

There are the Halna paper pots which are light, cheap and strong. Type L gives a staging life of about 4 weeks, while type H give a life of about 10 weeks with normal watering. The Hartmann fibre pots are a little cheaper on the whole and they last longer. We have had plants growing in them for about 16 weeks before they start to rot away. They are certainly tough and rigid, and under dry conditions they store indefinitely. There are also the Crop Pots which seem to be made of a type of reinforced cardboard clipped together, and they usually last about 6 months. These are made in two or three useful sizes. There are also the new reinforced Knightrider pots which seem much stronger than any other cardboard I have had as yet. They are light, unbreakable and last for a fair time.

The Care of Pots

It is unfortunate to report that clay pots often seem to collect green scum and moss, let alone mud and fungus growths. It is necessary, therefore, to be extremely careful with whatever pots are used, and to make certain that they are washed and scrubbed from time to time. Fortunately special flower pot brushes are available which fit exactly into the inside of a pot. They are circular in shape and it doesn't take a moment to twist them round and thus do the necessary from the bottom of the inside of the pot upwards. Three sizes are usually sold, one for the size 60's at about 3/6d. each; one for size 48's at say 4/0d. each; and one for the 32's at about 5/6d. each. There are also special brushes with 9- and 10-inch handles, which are not circular, but which are sold and used for scrubbing pots, and these retail at about 2/6d. each.

Always soak new pots thoroughly before using them—in fact on every occasion, when the pot is free, it should be given a thorough soaking in water and then be scrubbed well. It is better to use rain water on the whole than hard water. If the pots have got particularly dirty after they've been used for a number of years in the house, it may be necessary to use a special solution. This should consist of ¼ ounce of copper-carbonate and ¼ pint of ordinary household ammonia in a 2½ gallon bucketful of water. This will remove the most obdurate green algae or moss if a scrubbing brush is used with vigour. Be prepared to rinse the pots thoroughly in clean water after they have been treated with these chemicals.

Don't be temped to accept a present of some old, old pots that have been used for generations by some careless gardeners. Old pots that are almost encrusted with dirt and disease can easily be a menace rather than a blessing. If you are going to grow a few plants in the house, then it pays to have good pots. It is no good spending money on buying a first-class plant and then expecting it to grow well in a dirty cracked, Victorian specimen.

CHAPTER 3

THE COMPOST TO USE

YEARS ago, when I first started gardening and had to take the Royal Horticultural Society's examinations, it was necessary to learn twenty or thirty different potting mixtures, or composts as one learnt to call them, each one suited to a different kind of plant. For instance, the Begonias and Primulas might have a potting mixture consisting of 2 parts sand, 2 parts loam, 2 parts leafmould, ½ part of dried cow manure and a 5-inch flower pot full of bone meal to each bushel of this mixture made up. For the Azaleas and Ericas one used to use 2 parts of sand, 2 parts of loam, 2 parts of peatmoss, part of leafmould and a third of a part of cow manure, and so it went on.

It wasn't very easy always to go rushing about getting the dried cow manure! Many people who lived in the towns had no idea how this commodity could be obtained. It was a nuisance, to put it mildly, if you grew a large number of different kinds of plants, to have to be making up this mixture and then that mixture, in order to satisfy, as it was thought, the needs of differing plants.

Fortunately, however, for all pot plant growers, Mr. W. J. C. Lawrence, the Head of the Garden Research Department of the John Innes Horticultural Institution, and Mr. J. Newell, the Curator of the same Institution, got together and carried out some very significant experiments which showed that it was possible to grow a very large range of plants in one compost or, to put it another way, in one type of compost with modifications. After all, the plants need a soil which has a good moisture holding capacity, and one which is not only well-aerated but easily penetrated by the roots. It should grow in earth which contains a balanced supply of plant food and is free from all " evil " organisms.

The interesting thing about the various types of compost used in the olden days was the fact that gardener A would make up quite a different potting mixture to gardener B, and yet both would get quite good results. The fact was the one used heavy soil and lightened it with sand and peat, while another used light soil, added no sand, and plenty of peat. It has now been proved, as a result of a great many experiments, that what we need today are standard composts in which all kinds of widely differing types of plants can be grown.

It is no good attempting to use cow manure or leafmould, for no samples are alike, and both of them may possess undesirable qualities. One must introduce into the compost materials that can be standardised liked sedge peat, hoof and horn, superphosphates, sulphate of potash and ground limestone. The soil if possible must be sterilised. The method of composting must be simple. The cost of materials must be kept as low as possible.

Therefore one can say that the principles that must be laid down for the good standardised compost for pot plants should be as follows:

(1) That the potting soil must contain the necessary balanced food supply for the plants.

(2) That the strictest hygiene must be practised.

(3) That the compost should be in a good physical condition and possess the right crumbly structure for air to get in, and yet sufficient organic matter for moisture to be held.

(4) That the compost should contain loam, peat and sand in the right proportions.

(5) That the soil should be partially sterilised by heating to a minimum temperature of 180 degrees F. for not more than 30 minutes.

Having insisted on these 5 requirements, we must ensure that all the materials used are uniform in quality and that all of them are easy to get locally. Each material that is to be added to the potting compost should have a definite function. It should be there for one purpose and one purpose only. The keen pot plant grower should be able to make up exactly the same compost each time, and thus he should know that his plants will grow well, rather than just hope that they will. The loam used should be one which has grown good grass. The peat should be fibrous and must be of the sedge type. It should be clean and come from a well-known firm that caters specially for this purpose. The sand must be clean and sharp, and 60 per cent of the particles should be between a sixteenth and an eighth of a inch in size.

The John Innes Seed Compost (often called J.I.S.)

Those who are going to raise plants from seed sowing must make up a compost consisting of:

2 parts by bulk medium loam
1 part by bulk sedge peat
1 part by bulk coarse silver sand

add to each bushel of this mixture 1½ ounces of superphosphate and ¾ ounce of ground limestone or ground chalk.

By the way, a bushel of soil will exactly fill a box measuring 22 inches by 10 inches by 10 inches.

The John Innes Potting Compost (often called J.I.P.)

This consists of:

7 parts by bulk medium loam
3 parts by bulk good sedge peat
2 parts of bulk coarse silver sand

adding to each bushel of this mixture, 1½ ounces of hoof and horn meal (an eighth of an inch grist), 1½ ounces of superphosphate,* ¾ ounce of sulphate of potash, and ¾ ounce of ground limestone or chalk. (Known as John Innes 'Base')

Buying the Compost

There may be some reading this who by now have become "browned off." You are saying the Chapter started by

* Those who don't like using superphosphates can use powdered natural Rock Phosphates instead.

expressing the belief that simplification has been arrived at, and then from that time onwards the poor reader has been faced with J.I.S's, J.I.P's and what have you. Actually, of course, it is never possible to please everyone, and those who are really " keen " will want to know how to make up their own composts, and in justice I must cater for them. There are sure to be some readers, however, who live in towns, in flats, and who cannot possibly take the trouble to make up potting mixtures; and such will be glad to know that there are firms who provide these John Innes Potting Composts already prepared with absolutely the right ingredients. They supply these composts in hundredweights or in bushel or half-bushel bags, and anyone can be assured of getting the right scientific compost for the plants that he wishes to grow at home. I shall be pleased to supply any reader who has difficulty in getting the right compost locally with suitable names and addresses.

Actually, one can buy the hoof and horn, superphosphate and sulphate of potash* already made up from the horticultural chemist or horticultural sundriesman under the name " John Innes Base." For those who like to know an analysis, I would say that it should consist of 5·1 per cent nitrogen, 7·2 per cent soluble phosphoric acid, and 9·7 per cent potash.

One can omit the ground chalk or ground limestone in the case of plants which hate lime like the Azaleas and Ericas.

Don't just guess the quantities and say that's good enough. Be very careful to make certain that they are perfect in accordance with the formula that has been detailed.

If the peat arrives dry, as it usually does, wet it moderately before using it.

Mixing the Composts

Spread the loam out on the bench or floor an inch or two deep. Then spread the sedge peat evenly over the top and the sand on top of that. Hold back some of the sand if necessary to mix this with the fertilisers, as this makes it possible to apply them evenly over the area covered by the soil. Use a

* This can be a Sulphate of Potash made from Grape Skins.

spade or a trowel to turn the 3 layers (loam, sand and sedge peat) over and over, in order to make certain that they are thoroughly and properly mixed together.

Extra Food

Normally the compost which we have headed the "John Innes Potting Compost" is known as the J.I.P.1. It is indeed the standard potting compost which is used for the majority of plants. It contains the special John Innes Base which has been detailed purposely on page 16. Now if you add twice the quantity of John Innes Base in order to increase the amount of food put into the compost, you automatically make up what is known as the J.I.P.2, and if you add 3 times the quantity of John Innes Base, the J.I.P.3 is produced.

Therefore, one can say that when seeds are sown, the John Innes Seed Compost is used, but the two exceptions to this rule are the Cineraria and the *Solanum capsicastrum*, where the J.I.P.1 has proved to be far more useful. These plants are then grown on in the pots in which they flower and berry in the J.I.P.2. Most Primulas start their life in their 60's in the J.I.P.1 and are potted on into 48's in the J.I.P.2. The Citrus trees in pots do best in the J.I.P.3. Cyclamen prefer the J.I.P.2 whether in 60's or 48's. Chrysanthemums I always grow in the J.I.P.3 and ferns in the J.I.P.2.

Potting Compost for Cacti

Cacti should be grown in very open compost. The standard one, which the author has found satisfactory, consists of:

1 part by bulk good heavy loam
1 part by bulk coarse silver sand
1 part by bulk finely broken brick or powdered burnt clay
One sixteenth of granulated charcoal
One thirty-second of ground clean eggshell.

The Phyllocacti can do with a slightly richer compost, and so we usually add to the one detailed above, one part of sedge peat.

Some friends of mine who are keen cactus growers and verv expert, use the compost consisting of:

2 parts good loam
2 parts sharp silver sand
1 part broken flower pots into small pieces
½ part sedge peat

adding to each bushel of the mixture a 5-inch flower pot full of bone meal and a 5-inch flower pot full of ground limestone.

Hygiene

It's not much use taking infinite trouble to sterilise the soil used in the composts if the water taken in the greenhouse is allowed to become dirty, and so infected. Be sure then to scrub out the tanks, paint them with a 2 per cent solution of Formaldehyde to sterilise, and then fill with clean water and wash out. Then fill the tank once more.

Keep the potting bench absolutely clean. Never allow the plants to become overcrowded. Take away diseased plants before they infect others. Keep the panes of glass in the greenhouse perfectly clean so that the maximum of sunshine can get through. Control all pests by fumigation with the modern " smokes " in the evening, but more of this side of the work in Chapter 9.

Eclipse No-Soil Compost

Since this book was first written there has been introduced an excellent NO-SOIL Compost which amateurs find ideal for this purpose. There is no soil to sterilise and the compost arrives in a sealed bag ready to use. In the bag will be found the special plant foods that have to be added—in a similar way as in the case of the John Innes Compost on Page 16. It is possible by doubling and trebling the " doses " of food to alter the compost in exactly the same way as described under Extra Food on Page 18.

CHAPTER 4

PURCHASING THE PLANTS

No apology is made for having a short chapter on this subject. It certainly is short but very much to the point. The whole point of buying a pot plant is that it should give joy and pleasure over a long period. It's not like paying for a bunch of violets in Piccadilly Circus when you know perfectly well the flowers are not going to last for much more than three days.

Most people take a lot of trouble when spending money. A woman will stay hours and hours in a hat shop trying on this one and that one before she gets hold of the " creation " which she is sure is (a) of good value, and (b) suits her particular form of beauty. Yet, the same woman may easily just buy a pot plant from some huckster who comes to the front door and quite a high price may be asked for a plant that is of little or no value at all.

Year after year the same tricks are played by itinerant pedlars. There is the man for instance, who sells a wonderful climbing plant. It's going to grow and grow, he says, and bloom, and last for years. Actually, of course, the plant is an annual, usually *Ipomea purpurea,* which may grow fairly well for a month or two but, because it's an annual, it dies before the end of the year. I have known men sell Carnations in pots and describe them as perpetual flowering, when actually they are only Chabaud carnations and so just annuals that once again will only last a few months.

Make it a rule, therefore, never to buy plants at the door from men who do not know. Try, if you can, to buy from a Nurseryman who actually grows the plants and so knows (presumably) all about them. A bad grower will force his plants in order to make them large in the minimum of time. and he does this by giving them plenty of moisture and heat.

A good grower is one who will do everything possible to harden off the plants, so that they have as little heat as possible and lots of fresh air. Plants grown under these conditions are far happier when they are transferred to the rooms of a house.

Hardiness is tremendously important. The pot plant which will grow in a bedroom or sitting-room or even in the hall, must be so well hardened that it will be able to withstand the changes of temperature and even the inevitable little bit of draught that may occur from time to time in the house. Sometimes I am asked how the buyer can tell a properly hardened off plant and it isn't easy to give a perfect answer. One can say that the leaves should be clear and clean; the stems should be firm; the plant should look sturdy. There should be a general healthy look; but the final answer always is seen after the plant has been in the home for two or three days.

If you've been unlucky enough to buy a plant that has come out of a hot, moist greennouse, and so has been forced and is soft, you will find that after it has been in your room for a few days it will start to look miserable. The leaves may droop; the stems may go limp; and you will then think that the trouble is entirely due to your ill-treatment. Actually it may not be the case and so, when it does happen, do wonder whether the plant you bought was properly hardened off and discuss this very definitely with the supplier.

On the other hand, there are cases where it definitely is the buyer's mistake. The plant is taken home and given too much water. The plant is put on the mantelpiece above a roaring fire. A tender-leaved specimen is put on the hall table where it gets a nasty draught every time the front door opens. Do be kind to a newly-bought plant. Don't over-water it. In fact give it a minimum of water for the first few days. Put it where it will get the maximum amount of light during the day, but move it to the centre of the room at night time, so that it cannot be touched by the frost. If you take care of a plant, it may be that it will recover after its first set-back.

When buying evergreen plants, do make certain to see that none of the leaves are injured. In many cases the foliage just grows larger and larger, and if you start with a damaged leaf it will remain damaged almost for the rest of its life. Examine the plants carefully and see that there are no insect pests present. One day, a year or two back, I was called in to see a pot plant that a relation of mine had bought to discover why it wasn't doing well. The answer was very evident to the practised eye; hundred of aphides were congregated on the undersides of the leaves and sucking the sap.

Not only does it pay to turn the leaves over, but also to look down the stems to see if there are any scale insects. These, as their name suggests, are insects which have a scaly back and which stick so close to the stems or leaves that they may actually look part of them. They breed very quickly, so you don't want to introduce them into the house. Another pest which can give trouble is the Red Spider (see page 56). This is not, curiously enough, red in colour, nor is it large like the ordinary spiders we think about. Actually it's a tiny little mite which can only be seen with a magnifying glass and which collects in large numbers underneath the leaves, where there is the tiniest form of cobwebbing. Leaves which are attacked in this way are usually yellow or brown in colour and the plants are stunted. A pocket magnifying glass is useful when looking for this pest.

Don't necessarily go for the very large plants. There is always the danger that they may have been forced, and if you buy a huge specimen you haven't got the joy of watching it grow. Get hold of a sturdy, well-grown, hardy young plant, and have the joy of watching it grow larger and larger. Only when it's absolutely necessary to brighten up the corner of a room immediately need a fully grown plant be bought.

Beginners' Choice

Some reading this may say, " I'm the veriest beginner and I would like to know the names of one or two really simple plants that I cannot go wrong with. Give me the names of just a few plants, one perhaps of each type, which I could start with and then, because I have succeeded, I would be encouraged to go on and on." As a climber, I can strongly recommend *Ficus pumila*, commonly known as the Climbing

MONSTERA DELICIOSO

AN EXTREMELY USEFUL PLANT IN THE HOME. NOTICE ITS FASCINATING CUT LEAVES.

CODIAEUM VARIEGATUM
A BEAUTIFUL BUT RATHER MORE DIFFICULT PLANT.

Fig. Grow it in the J.I.P.3* It will climb enthusiastically, producing masses of heart-shaped leaves with wavy margins. It doesn't bear any flowers. For a flowering plant there is a lot to be said for *Impàtiens Hòlstii*, a relation of the Garden Balsam. It produces lovely flowers with spurs on them. The stems go on blooming until late in the autumn and the plants can be pruned back quite hard in the early spring. Grow it in the J.I.P.3.*

Maybe you'd like to have a hanging plant. In this case, start with *Saxifraga sarmentosa,* sometimes called the Strawberry Geranium, and other times wrongly called the Strawberry Begonia. Actually it's a synonym of *Saxifraga stolonifera.* I have heard it called Mother of Thousands, Roving Sailor and Aaron's Beard. The flowers are white, the two inner petals having yellow spots at the base and the centre petals red spots at the base. These are seen during the months of July and August. It is a plant that will survive in poor soil and in a cold spot. It is a good window plant.

For those who just want one plant which is far better than an Aspidistra and which can start by being in the dining-room or drawing-room, and then when it gets larger can be put at the foot of the staircase, where it will grow into a beautiful little tree, there is nothing easier than *Grevillea robusta,* commonly known as the Silk Oak. The shoots are silvery and downy, and in young plants the leaves are often 1 ft. long. The flowers are golden yellow, though I have never seen them in this country.

Start, of course, with one or two good plants, and then gradually increase your collection. Study Chapters 10 to 16 carefully and decide which specimens you would like to have, and maybe tell your relations and friends, who should be delighted to think that at long last the " present problem " in your case has at least been solved. Gifts of plants are always very welcome indeed!

* See page 18.

CHAPTER 5

TAKING CARE OF THE PLANTS

It is a good thing to start by picturing the plant as it really is. When saying this, I am reminded of the story of the lost donkey and the boy who found it. When asked how he found it, he said, " I fancied I was a donkey, and then I thought to myself, where would I go, and I went to that place, and the donkey was there." Try and put yourself therefore in the place of the plant.

The soil in which you were growing is completely cut off from the great bulk of soil in the earth. You are isolated. You are in a room in which it never rains. Your leaves are never damped by the morning and evening dew. You may not receive the direct rays of sunshine. You don't breathe the " balmy " air of the out of doors but maybe only the foetid atmosphere of the living room.

When all the moisture in the ball of soil has been used up by your roots, there is no more to draw on and, in fact, the ball of soil in which you are growing shrinks, so much so that there's quite a space between the rim of the ball and the inside rim of the pot. The room may get very hot during the day owing to a fire, and very cold during the night owing to the frost. Children may easily move you from one spot to another.

You are badgered about from pillar to post, on the dining room table one day, on the windowsill the next, and perched precariously on the mantelpiece a week later. Sometimes you are nobody's care, and another day everybody seems to bother about you. The mother of the home gives you water in the morning, the daughter in the afternoon, and when father comes home at night he gives you a drop. Thus some days your roots are swimming in a pool, and other days they are as dry as dust. There seems to be no continuity at all.

Eventually you grow too large for your pot. You've exhausted every bit of plant food and you even seem to have started eating the soil. Nobody ever thinks of re-potting you into a bigger pot, and so you starve; or it may be that you ought to have an autumn rest, and be laid on your side for a bit to dry off, but nobody helps and you are expected to go on and on producing leaves and flowers without any stop at all. Usually people forget that you need any sort of food at all. They never think of buying a bottle of Liquinure and giving you this from time to time. It's a poor life and it's no wonder that, after struggling along for a few months, you give up the ghost and die.

I have purposely put all this in the personal tense because of a very great desire to bring home the many points, which have, I hope, been put into their right perspective. Plants are living "creatures," they breathe and they drink, and they need food. If they are going to be taken out of their natural environment, then they must have special care and attention. Water must be given exactly when it is necessary. The leaves may need syringing over, or even wiping over with clean water if the room gets very dusty. Food will have to be given from time to time. In fact, plants have to be cared for just like children. Fortunately they don't run about, and so they are always to be found where they are put, but this doesn't mean to say that they can be neglected. Read on and see how best you may take care of your plants, for all the important points are stressed under separate headings.

Air

One of the great mistakes that beginners make with a greenhouse is that they don't open the ventilators enough, and so often those who grow pot plants feel that they oughtn't to open the windows because the air will injure their precious specimens. Always open the windows during the day, even in the winter, and don't mind having a window open at night time in the summer (apart from the fear of burglars!). There is all the difference between good, clean, fresh air and a draught. Don't, therefore, have a window open *and* the door, with the plant on the table mid-way. Wind blowing on the leaves of the plants causes them to transpire moisture unnecessarily.

Plants growing on the windowsills may be killed by frosts in the winter, but usually they are " murdered " by bitter, cold draughts, because the window itself doesn't fit snugly and tightly on to the sill. Remember, then, that it isn't coldness that causes the trouble, it's draught. So do everything you can to prevent nasty cold draughts in a room.

Direct Light

If the leaves of the plants are to do their work properly, they must have light. It is the green colouring matter in the leaves which enables the plant to get hold of the energy from the sunlight, and thus to marry the carbon in the air with the oxygen and hydrogen which it sends up from its roots as water. It is this unifying process which produces the carbohydrates. When lecturing to the students at The Horticultural Training College, Thaxted, this process is called photosynthesis. Thus the plants help human beings, for they take the carbon-dioxide in and, having absorbed the carbon, they breathe out again the oxygen they do not need. We who need the oxygen are naturally delighted.

One of the reasons, therefore, why we often grow our plants on the windowsill is that they may get the direct sunlight and thus manufacture the carbon they need. If, on the other hand, they cannot get direct light, they will be satisfied with reflected light, and that is the reason why plants in the modern rooms which are distempered or painted in light colours do far better, than plants growing in rooms which are, say, panelled with dark oak.

I suppose if we lived for our plants entirely and didn't mind a bit how we suffered, we should arrange for the rooms to be nice and warm during the day, and then from about tea-time onwards we should allow the atmosphere to get cooler and cooler so that by midnight they were at about 40 degrees F. One doesn't want the room to fall below the freezing point at any time. It will help, therefore, if those who have central heating turn down their radiators when they go to bed, so that the rooms will get a little cooler. It will help, also, if those who have no central heating adopt one of the modern fuel-saving grates, so that with a little " nutty " slack the fire just smoulders quietly during the night.

Don't try and force the plants along during the winter. Most of them like a rest, and they refuse to grow strongly during the weeks when they should be allowed to " mark time." Those who have to leave their plants in cold rooms during the night, and who fear that they may be touched by the frost, should put a sheet or two of newspaper over their plants before they go to bed. It is wonderful what protection newspaper will give, and it doesn't seem to matter whether it's *The Times* or *The Daily Worker*! Aim, though, if you can, for no really serious drop in temperature at any time of the day.

Lastly, when considering warmth, remember that there are plants which are hardier than others, and so study the Chapters 10 to 14, and choose specimens which are obviously suited to the different rooms of the house. You may need a Silk Oak (*Grevillea robusta*) for the hall, an *Echinops Cactus* for the spare room, which will almost look after itself, while for the sitting-room, which is constantly in use, choose a plant like a Philodendron.

Water and Watering

Most people ruin plants by over-watering, especially during the wintertime. It is far better to wait until the soil in the pots is *nearly* dry (do please note this word " nearly "), and then give a good watering, than just to give drips and drabs every hour or two. It is when over-watering is done that the air is driven out of the soil, and this prevents the bacteria from functioning as they should. Remember that the earth in the pots should be filled with thousands of living organisms that are going to work and help you produce a beautiful plant.

Of course there are one or two plants like the Cyperus which will not mind excess moisture, and with such the plan is to stand the pot in a saucer of water all the time. In the normal way, however, plants should never be watered in this manner, because when the soil is too wet the roots rot and die. One of the signs of a plant suffering in this way is that the leaves go limp and droop. The harassed plant owner then thinks that the specimen is suffering from lack of moisture and gives more water, and so only emphasises the trouble.

One of the reasons why it is important to keep the leaves of plants clean, either by syringing them over from time to time with water to imitate dew, or by wiping them carefully with soft water, is to remove the dust which may easily block up the breathing pores and so prevent the foliage from taking in the carbon-dioxide it needs. It isn't only the leaves, however, that have to be considered; there is the soil itself, for if a plant is stood on the windowsill on a hot day, the compost in the pot may easily get baked and the roots of the plant will thus suffer.

Plants that normally like a little shade don't want to be put in full sun. Plants that like plenty of sun on their leaves but a nice cool root run, will appreciate the use of sedge peat put on to the tops of the pots, so as to act as a buffer between the sunshine above and the soil below. Never allow the soil in a pot to bake—on hot sunny days, pot plants can go into the centre of the room as they can during a cold frosty night. Remember that light is all right, but sun heat may be all wrong, and so often we confuse the two. Furthermore the sun blazing down through a window may cause scorching, whereas the sun beating down on a plant in the open may not have the same effect.

There is one little point with regard to the plants with variegated leaves that ought to be mentioned. It is the green colouring matter, or chlorophyll, in the leaf which can carry out the carbon manufacture. Where leaves are mottled or variegated there is naturally far less chlorophyll, and so such plants should have more direct sunlight than those which have foliage that is wholly green. In fact, I have known plants which started life with beautiful variegations turn dark green in a home because they were never given enough sunlight; the owners of these plants were very surprised when I insisted on putting them back on the windowsill, but in ten days or a fortnight the beautiful yellow variegations appeared once more.

Warmth

It is wonderful the way that plants will acclimatise themselves to the warmth of a particular room. It is not correct to say that because a plant seems to insist on 70 degrees F. in the greenhouse of The Horticultural College, that it must have that amount of heat in the house. Of course, in a cooler room the plant may not grow quite so large, but it may be just as beautiful, and in fact more dainty or precious. The interesting thing with plants is that they can put up with more heat if they get more light, but generally speaking in our homes they get more heat during the winter months when we have fires, and that is just the time, as a rule, when they get less light. Remember these facts when you are looking after your plants during the winter-time, and do try and bring about the right conditions as nearly as possible, so that your plants will succeed.

Syringing and Watering

When dealing with important points of watering on page 27 it was mentioned that it is important to keep the leaves of plants clean. Much can be done to this end by the use of a syringe. A plant can be stood on the windowsill just outside the window, and then the syringe with plenty of clean water can be used with good effect (just be careful about the drops falling on the heads of passers-by below). In the cold wintry days this may not be possible and the alternative is to put the plant into the bath and syringe it there. If you don't want to buy a syringe, it is possible to hold the plant carefully by putting the fingers over the ball of soil, and then allowing the leaves to be under a dripping tap. Anyway I feel sure that pot plant owners will use some ingenuity to make certain that the leaves get a good wash.

Plants with very large leaves, as was suggested on page 28 can easily be wiped over with a clean damp rag, or with cotton wool, or even with a nice soft sponge. There are problems when you come to spray the leaves of a plant climbing up a wall. The answer here may be to hold a piece of plywood at the back, or not to attempt to do the spraying, but to wash each individual leaf. I had an aunt who always got out of the difficulties of syringing plants by standing them out in the yard or porch and letting the rain do its work naturally.

This idea of standing the plants outside for a bit does no harm at all. Furthermore, of course, rain water never marks the leaves, which chalky mains water may do. The only snag is in regard to the plants that need a fairly high temperature, like the Crotons or Dracaenas; these must not be allowed to get cold and, further, any moisture that does get on to their leaves must dry off before sunset. The other danger concerns the very hairy-leaved specimens. These tend to rot off if the water is heavy on the foliage. You get the same kind of thing taking place in the rock garden during the winter with the Androsaces.

Regular Meals?

It isn't possible to lay down a kind of weekly "Menu" for feeding pot plants. All one can do is generalise and to make it quite clear that taking it by and large plants need to be fed during the spring and summer and may want very little from say the beginning of October to the end of March. It is no good trying to force them into growth when there is a minimum of light. This ties up perfectly with the suggestions made on page 29 with regard to warmth. Of course there are some flowering plants which produce their blooms in the winter, and they are the exception that proves the rule. Chrysanthemums, for instance, may be fed in the winter months with profit to the grower.

It must be remembered that all plants take in their foods by means of soil moisture, and so it is convenient to apply the nitrogen, phosphates, potash and other trace elements in a liquid form. It is possible to buy specially prepared liquid manure in bottles. This being sold under the name "Liquinure." This concentrated plant food can then be diluted in accordance with the instruction given on the container, and the soil in the pots can thus be "fed." Normally speaking plants will only need such a tonic once every ten days. The amount that is given will depend on the size of the plant. An 8-inch pot, for instance, might easily need ¼ of a pint of the diluted Liquinure. A 3-inch pot, on the other hand, will be happy to have less than 2 tablespoonfuls.

The plants that grow more rapidly will need more food than plants that grow slowly. Climbers for instance, like the *Cobaea scandens*, need feeding once a week or so, once they really get going. On the other hand, the majority of the Cacti need no Liquinure at all. It is equally true to say that when you first pot up a young plant, there should be sufficient plant food in the John Innes compost to last for a couple of months or so. Even when plants are re-potted, they seldom want feeding for two months because the tiny root hairs are sure to have got broken. It takes some time before the plant can re-adjust itself to its new conditions.

Some people have found a poor plant flagging, and looking miserable, and have made the great mistake of jumping to the idea that this is through lack of food. As I have tried to point out under the heading Watering, very often such a condition is found because of too much water and not too little. Therefore, to attempt to feed a plant which is already "sick" through soddenness by giving it unnecessary food will merely cause further "plant indigestion." On the other hand, don't feed with dilute Liquinure when the soil is absolutely dry, or this may cause scorching to the root hairs.

Probably the best time for feeding is in the evening. This will give the roots a chance of absorbing the plant food gradually, which is far better than expecting it to "gobble" down a sudden dose in the middle of the day. Remember that a plant only needs very little food, and thus be careful never to give an overdose. Double doses do more harm than good. Your aim as a careful gardener must be to feed from time to time, and with most plants this is, as I have already said, once every ten days, though with strong growers in the spring and summer once every Saturday night is quite a good idea.

Those who have plants which are 7 or 8 years of age can

do much to help matters from the point of view of food by removing each early spring the top soil of the pot to a depth of say 1½ inches. The work has to be done very carefully indeed so as to disturb the roots as little as possible. I always use a small kitchen fork when working among the roots to remove the depth of soil. In its place the Potting Compost No. 2 or 3, depending on circumstances, will be put into position and pressed down firmly. This kind of work is always done in cases where it is not desired to re-pot the plant into a larger pot.

Staking and Trimming

If it is necessary to stake a plant, do this work so that the effect really looks natural. Don't make the mistake of using one bamboo and then tying up the plant roughly to this, so that it looks like " a sack of potatoes." Splitting a bamboo into 3 or 4 pieces is quite a good idea, and one of these " splits " may then be used for each flowering stem and can be put into the pot, if necessary, sloping slightly outwards. Always use a stake that is longer than will be required eventually, for it can always be cut back a little once the plant has grown to its fullest length, and it is desired to make the stakes as inconspicuous as possible.

When using stakes, it is useful to make the actual tie with the green cotton twine made especially for this purpose. Because it is green, it is inconspicuous, and because of its special manufacture it is strong. Such special tying material is sold under the name of " Nutscene Twill " or Twist.

With the feathery plants, it is possible to use twiggy sticks like the tops of pea sticks. These are pushed into the pot when the plants are young, and the stems then grow in and among them. They are more usually employed in the case of annuals which are being grown from seed.

In most cases where you are growing climbing plants, you will probably not want to have them climbing up the walls or round the windows. The climbers that do not grow too rampantly are usually quite happy growing up a little trellis-work stuck in the pot. This can be made very easily. A cane can be split in two to make the two uprights (a cane about 18 inches in length should be right for a five-inch pot). These two uprights can then be pushed down the sides of the pots, in lines with the sides, forming a sort of open V. Now two or three cross-pieces can be tied to the two uprights to form the trellis-work. If you can manage to paint the split canes green and tie the joints with green twist, then the plant will blend in much better with the framework.

Don't forget to cut off the yellowing leaves as and when they appear, and the dead flowers. Broken stems should be pruned back with a sharp knife. This is a job to do once a week, or at any rate when the plants get their syringing or sponging.

CHAPTER 6

THE FUN OF PROPAGATION

THE Chapter has purposely been headed "The Fun of Propagation " because those who are growing pot plants need not think that they must set out to increase the stock of the plants they have already. There is absolutely no need to do this. There are plenty of nurserymen who are experts on the subject, and will be only too delighted to supply further plants as and when necessary. Furthermore, it isn't always possible in a small flat or " bed-sit " to do such work. On the other hand, it really is great fun trying to raise your own plants and somehow, when you are able to say " I struck that plant myself," that ivy, or whatever it may be, is far more your own.

Plants can be propagated in various ways. There are stem cuttings, root cuttings and leaf cuttings. Some plants throw little " runners " which start to root in their parent's pot; These can easily be severed and then planted into a little pot of their own. With many of the ferns and other foliage plants, division is a simple method—merely a question of knocking the plant out of the pot, and then dividing it up into a number of smaller portions and re-potting each division in its John Innes Potting Compost. It is also possible to raise a number of plants from seeds; whilst layering is sometimes carried out.

Seed Sowing

It isn't always possible to cope with numbers of seed pans or boxes in a house or flat, but the advantage of the method is that the baby plants do get used to room conditions in their early stages. The bigger the seed, of course, the easier the work. Most people have had success with orange and apple pips, for instance, and with climbing Nasturtium seeds. The seeds of the *Ipomoea pestigridis* are large, as also are those of the *Albizzia lophantha*. This is the plant which is sometimes used for sub-tropical bedding, and produces a mop-like cluster of bright pink stamens. Anyway, whatever seeds are bought, they have to be examined first, and the general rule is to sow them about 3 times deeper than their actual size.

Some seeds have quite hard coats. This is particularly true in the case of the darker colours of sweet peas. All hard-coated seeds are best soaked for 24 hours in warmish water. It helps, too, if the skin of the seed is nipped with a sharp knife, so as to allow the water to penetrate. After the soaking treatment, the seeds may be sown in the J.I. Seed Compost and, when germination takes place, it is well to select the strongest plants only, discarding the others. Once the plants have been raised, of course, what happens depends entirely on the raiser. Climbers can be put into larger pots, so as to clamber up the wall or windowsill. An alternative is to grow them in bowls and allow them to hang down like long trails or ropes. I have done this with Nasturtiums and it has been very effective. Specimen plants will, of course, be potted up singly.

In the case of the smaller seeds, the general rules are drawn from nature. The seeds are distributed over the surface of the ground and usually fall about the same time as the leaves do; and so are not covered so deeply. Baby seeds in pans are often not covered at all, or just have the slightest quantity of fine compost sifted over through a fine sieve. It is quite a good idea to mix fine seed with fine sand. This helps to get an even distribution. With such baby seed it is usually better to water the compost before sowing rather than afterwards. After sowing, the box or pan should be covered with a sheet of glass and then a sheet of brown paper. The glass prevents the compost from drying out too quickly and the darkness encourages root formation. The moment the seeds germinate, the glass and paper should be removed.

The pots or pans which are used for seed sowing must always be very thoroughly crocked. That is to say, plenty of broken pieces of pot must be put into the base of the container, and some sedge peat over that, the whole idea being to ensure that the drainage is perfect. The John Innes Seed Compost is always placed on top of this drainage material and is firmed with a flat " presser " (see drawing) made specially for the purpose. The surface of the compost must be level and just firm before the seeds are sown.

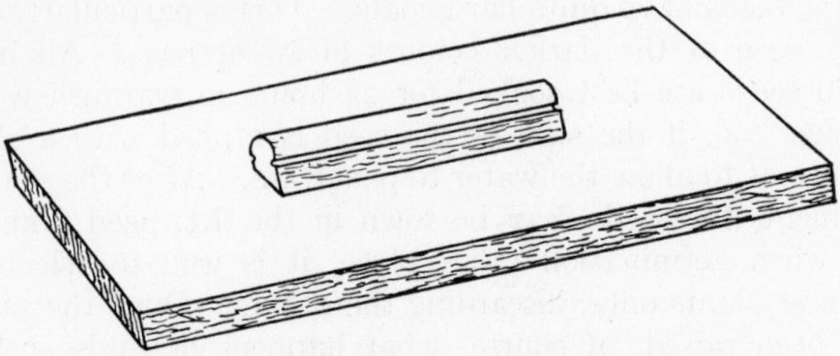

A flat wooden presser for pressing down compost in boxes and leaving it level.

Once the seedlings are through, they may be transplanted into little pots containing the John Innes Potting Compost 1 and here they are allowed to grow quietly. It is always better to transplant when they are tiny than to wait until they get too large. From the smaller pot, they can in turn be potted up into the larger pot in which they are to grow, and more of this side of the work is discussed in the following Chapter.

Remember that there is not much point in raising your own plants from seed unless the seedlings are going to look attractive and you are going to get a good deal of pleasure during the " growing up " period. I wouldn't, for instance, advise somebody without a greenhouse to try and raise Primulas, Cyclamen or Cinerarias. It is much more satisfactory to buy the plants when they've been grown to a fair size.

Division

When carrying out any method of vegetative propagation. you can ensure that the plants propagated will be true to type—which of course you never can in the case of seeds. But plants propagated vegetatively are more prone to disease. The great advantage, however, of this method is that quick results are achieved.

Remember with division that the outside portions of the clump are the youngest parts, and so more vigorous. Certainly retain these, even if it is necessary to discard the centre portions. The best time for splitting up a plant is usually early in the spring, or in the autumn. It sometimes helps if a little John Innes P.C.1 is worked into the centre of a clump it is proposed to divide some weeks before the actual work is done. This tends to encourage new growth. Of course one can only split up a plant which grows in such a manner as to make this possible. Aspidistras are the easiest example. The French love their Sansevierias and split these up from time to time. In this case the work is usually done from the middle of February to the end of April. Saxifrages can be divided in the spring, so can those dwarf and ornamental plants known as Chlorophytum. However, in Chapters 10 to 16 care has been taken to make it quite clear which method of propagation is advised in the case of each genus described.

Cuttings

Most plants can be propagated by cuttings. There are root cuttings, tip cuttings, leaf cuttings, soft wood cuttings, hard wood cuttings, stem cuttings, heel cuttings and so on. All cuttings, of course, should be taken from healthy plants, and any cuts made should always be done with a really sharp-bladed knife, which is not only straight but clean.

Hardwooded cuttings are usually taken from the shrubby plants in October. They are about 8 inches long and it helps matters if they are taken with a small heel, that is to say with a tiny little piece of the old wood or bark at the base. Such cuttings can be struck in a deep box, covered with a sheet of glass. This should have plenty of drainage holes at the bottom, and over these a layer of rough sedge peat at least an inch deep should be placed. On top of this should be a 2 or 3 inch layer of coarse silver sand and the cuttings are dibbled into this material. Also the box should be deep enough so that when the sheet of glass is put on the top, the leaves will not be disturbed. The sand should be watered regularly with tepid water to keep it just moist, and only when the cuttings have rooted should the glass be removed.

If you are propagating any of the true acid-loving plants like the heaths, azaleas and rhododendrons, then it is better to use pure sedge peat perhaps without any sand at all, or with a mixture consisting of 3 parts sedge peat and 1 part silver sand. It helps greatly with the hardwood cuttings if the bases are dipped in a hormone solution before they are

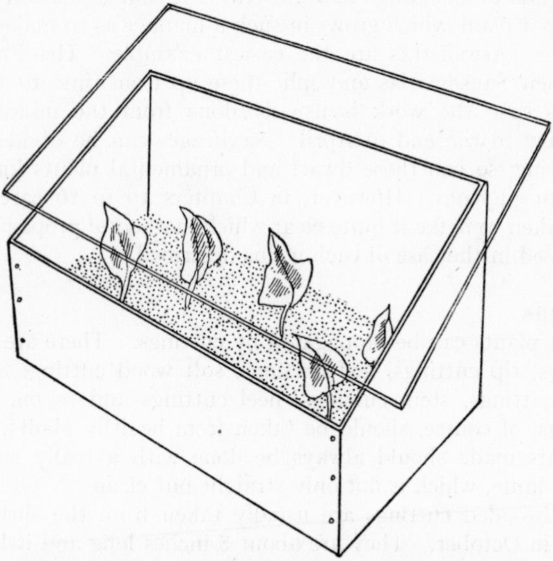

Another type of propagating box with sloping sides. Fill it 4–6 inches deep with sharp silver sand or vermiculite.

pushed into the sand or peat. Some people prefer to use the hormone powders instead, and these are certainly excellent for stimulating root growth. If you consult your local horticultural chemist or horticultural sundriesman on the subject, he will supply you with exactly what is needed.

If you are lucky enough to be able to buy an old accumulator jar from a junk shop, this might be used instead of a box, but the disadvantage is that it has no drainage, so we have to put into the bottom plenty of crocks and about a 3-inch depth of sedge peat before the soil and sand is put on the top. If it is necessary to stand such a propagating case in the sun, because of warmth, then it is advisable to use a strip of butter muslin over the outside to act as a kind of curtain, and to break up the rays of the sun. Cuttings, when trying to strike roots, do not like direct sun's rays. They like moisture and warmth, however.

MINIATURE ELECTRICALLY-HEATED PROPAGATING FRAME

There are today on the market a number of miniature propagating frames, in which it is possible to produce many of the required conditions for germinating seed or striking cuttings. Some of them are just large enough to take one seed box, but others can take two or three. They are usually heated by an electric light bulb, and by varying the wattage of the bulb, the temperature can be increased or decreased. The whole affair is usually rather like a large box, with the top and tops of the sides in glass. The electric light bulb is in a compartment at the bottom and is below a metal tray in which the seed box or small pots can be stood. In some models the tray can be flooded, so that the box or pots can be watered from underneath. The atmosphere can be regulated by opening or closing the glass top. These little miniature frames or greenhouses are very suitable for the home, as they take up little space and only need " plugging in ".

Soft Wood Cuttings

The soft wood cuttings are usually taken in June and July, and may be struck in the home-made propagating case advised above. In this instance, though, the case should be placed so that it receives the whole sun. The cuttings are just pushed into the sand and watered regularly. In very hot weather, in fact, they may have to be watered every hour! It always helps if the baby propagating case has a little bottom heat, but this should never be overdone. Cuttings may easily be struck

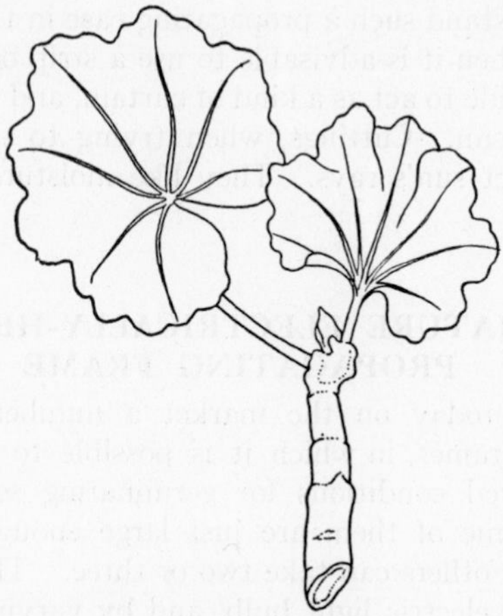

A soft wood cutting.

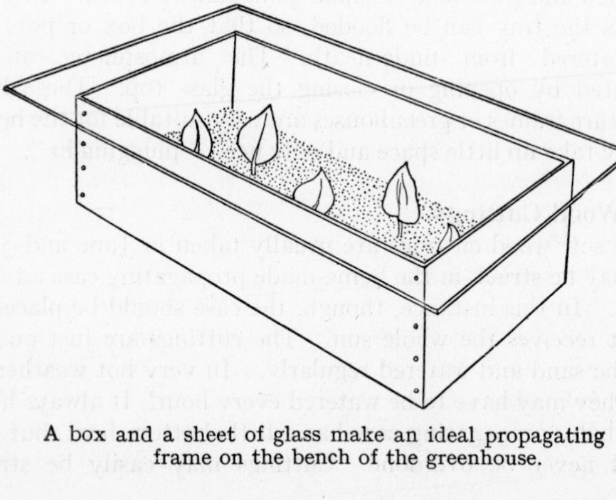

A box and a sheet of glass make an ideal propagating frame on the bench of the greenhouse.

around the edge of a pot if desired, rather than in an actual box.

Cuttings need not be very long. In fact, the smaller they are, on the whole, the quicker they start. If the stems are not much thicker than 2 pins held together, then the cutting need only be an inch or so in length. When the stems are twice as thick as this, they may be two inches in length, whereas if it necessary to strike a cutting whose stem is the thickness of a normal pencil, then the cutting might easily be 6 inches in length. Aim, however, to keep the cutting small, rather than large. I say this because most people err on the large side.

A cut should be made just below a node, there is the little swelling where the leaves arise, and the two or three lower

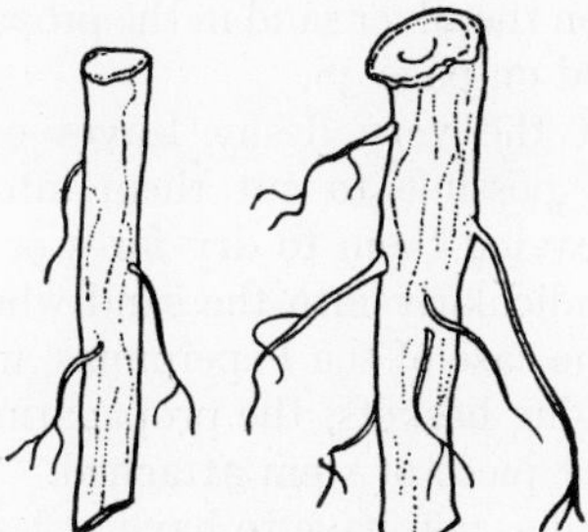

Typical root cuttings.

leaves should be removed. It helps if the base of this cutting is then pushed into the sand or peat, rather than for a hole to be made for it first with a dibber. It is so important that the base of the cutting should actually be resting firmly on the material in which its roots are to grow.

Root Cuttings

Plants which have nice thick roots may be propagated in this way. Small portions of the root are chosen, anything from 1 to 2 inches in length. Care must be taken to plant the part of the root which is nearest the stem uppermost. The top of the cuttings should be cut level and the base to a point. This specially prepared root cutting should then be buried in the

John Innes Seed Compost, so that the top is covered to a depth of $\frac{1}{2}$ inch.

Leaf Cuttings

One of the most interesting ways of propagating plants is by means of their leaves. This is of course a particularly useful method because it saves removing shoots. It is excellent with the fleshy-leaved plants, but not quite so simple with leaves that are very thin. To get the best results, the leaves must be treated in various ways. For instance in the case of Begonias, it always helps if the veins of the leaves are cut through, but in such a manner that the cuts do not penetrate to the other side. The leaves with their cut side downwards are then laid flat on the silver sand in the propagating box which has been described on page 38.

In the case of the very fleshy leaves of plants like the Sansevieria, it is possible to cut them into 4 or 5 sections and then, after leaving them to dry for 3 or 4 days, they can be pushed perpendicularly into the sand where they will root quite well. In the case of the Peperomias, many of which are excellent for hanging baskets, the propagating is best done by a leaf with a short piece of stem attached. With the African Violet or Saintpaulia, you have to have at least an inch of leaf stalk at the base when this is inserted into the sand. The sand in this case should not be too wet.

Cuttings in Water

Many home growers of pot plants have been fascinated to find that some cuttings, especially the Ivies, seem to throw out roots quite happily in water. There are two rules which must be borne in mind; one is that the vase used must be opaque—if you use clear glass, roots are not produced quickly, as they are hindered by the light; two, that a narrow-necked vase, for some reason or another, seems to give better results than one which is very wide at the top. Here the plan is to allow the cutting to have its bottom an inch or two in water, and of course there must be at least one bud on the length of stem which is immersed.

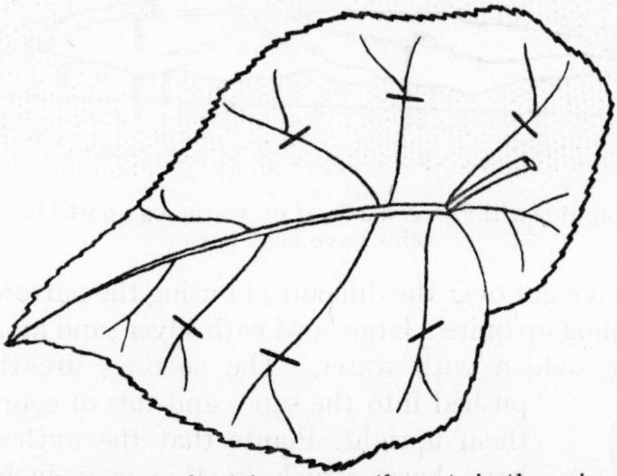

A begonia leaf cutting—note the cuts in the veins
(*see* page 42).

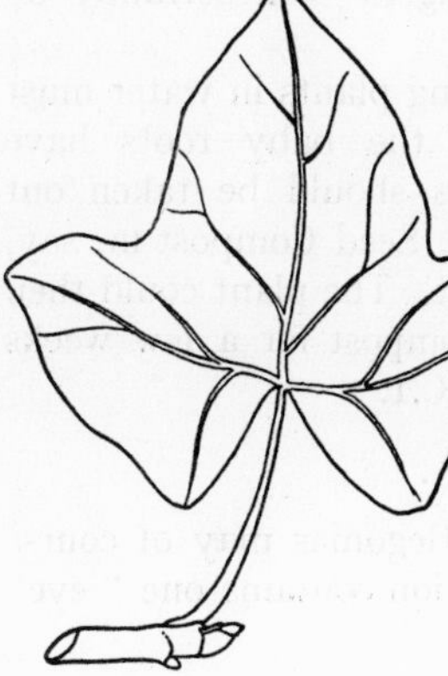

An Ivy leaf cutting.

Another type of leaf cutting.

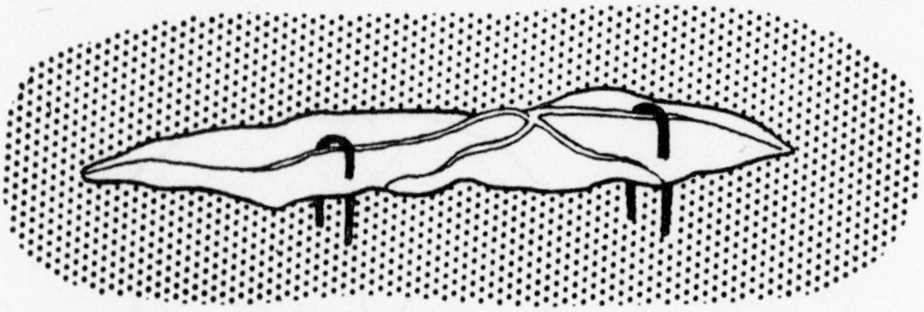

Pegging down the Begonia Leaf on to the compost after the veins have been cut.

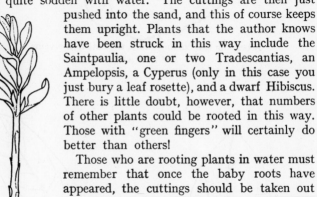

Some have got over the difficulty of using the narrow-necked vase by filling up quite a large bowl with silver sand and making this quite sodden with water. The cuttings are then just pushed into the sand, and this of course keeps them upright. Plants that the author knows have been struck in this way include the Saintpaulia, one or two Tradescantias, an Ampelopsis, a Cyperus (only in this case you just bury a leaf rosette), and a dwarf Hibiscus. There is little doubt, however, that numbers of other plants could be rooted in this way. Those with "green fingers" will certainly do better than others!

A Tip Cutting.

Those who are rooting plants in water must remember that once the baby roots have appeared, the cuttings should be taken out for potting up into J.I. Seed Compost in, say, a small 60 or thumbpot. The plant could then be grown on in this compost for a few weeks before it is transferred into the J.I.P.C.1.

Tubers

Plants having tuberous roots like Begonias may of course be cut into pieces, providing each portion contains one "eye" or bud.

CHAPTER 7

POTTING ON

THE time comes, of course, when some plants need a little more room in which to spread their roots. The amateur finds it difficult to decide when re-potting is really necessary, and in order to help him I would say right away that with the normal slow-growing pot plants it is seldom necessary to do anything about it for two or three years. Those who are growing cactus plants will find that they can remain in their pots for six or seven years, though in this case they may like a little renewal of the top inch or so. With the Sansevierias, the old head gardeners used to say that you must leave the plants in the pots until the roots actually smash the earthenware, and that only under these conditions that perfect plants would be produced.

As against this, of course, there are very quick-growing plants like the Eucalyptus, which may have to be re-potted three times a year. This is, however, an exception. If you buy a small Cyclamen, then of course this will be re-potted after the corm has had its resting period. No one bothers to re-pot annuals, of course, because they die at the end of the season. Bulbs, too, are just knocked out of their pots after the foliage has died down and passed back all the manufactured plant food.

We are, therefore, in this Chapter dealing with very general principles. The idea is to cope with the plants which are perennial and which will go on growing, however slowly, year after year. Care has been taken to deal specifically with the normal propagation of the plants in Chapter 10, 11 and 12. Here we have to give the necessary pointers which will enable the flat-dweller to know what he must do when the time comes for "potting on."

It is so easy to be misled by the way plants behave. For instance, if you have been over-watering, the leaves of the plants will flag and look very unhappy. Somebody may come along to you and suggest that some sort of re-potting should be done. Again, plants can look extremely " poorly " if they are not watered properly, or if they have not been fed. Therefore don't jump to the conclusion that it is necessary to re-pot without carrying out some examination of the roots.

Place the fingers of one hand over the soil at the top of the pot, and then turn the pot upside down. Knock the rim gently on the edge of the table, and by this tapping the ball of soil should come out without any difficulty. Make certain, of course, that the plant has been watered normally, because if it is absolutely dry, then the roots will come out of the pot in a cloud of dust and sand. The idea is that you should be able to knock out the ball of the soil in one piece without it breaking up at all. Now examine it carefully, and if the network of roots seems to have completely " eaten up " all the soil in the pot, then you will know that re-potting time has come.

There are always exceptions to every rule. It is very difficult to handle a prickly cactus in this way, and the only thing you can do here is to crack the pot and just waste it. Fortunately a cactus doesn't want to be re-potted very often! In the case of plants that have dried off, of course you shouldn't water, because the whole idea is just to knock the bulb or corm or whatever it may be out of its pot in a dry condition.

Your next job is to re-pot the plant into a container which is not more than one third larger. Go to your retailer and ask for the next larger size in pots, and you will be able to see which this is from the drawings and descriptions in Chapter 2. The new pot should be soaked in water before it is used, or, if you are lucky enough to get one second-hand, thoroughly scrubbed with warm water first; and if it comes from an unknown source, it should be steeped in a 2 per cent solution of formaldehyde for at least half an hour before being washed and cleaned. It should then be stood in a sunny place where it will dry off naturally.

You should also examine the roots of the knocked-out plant and, if any of them are diseased, prune these back carefully with a sharp knife to the point where they are obviously healthy. Next tackle the mass of tangled roots which denotes that the plant is root-bound, and tease these out with a pencil. Remove any of the soil there may be from the pot, but don't attempt to knock any of the other earth away. Also take away the crocks which will be found at the bottom of the ball of soil, and use clean new ones in the new pot.

Some plants, such as the Asparagus Ferns, produce what look like little tubers, which are usually white in colour. Don't attempt to cut these off, because they store plant food. All members of the Legume family (i.e. the plants which have flowers similar in shape to the Sweet Pea) have little white nodules on their roots. These are the nitrogenous bacteria which live in symbiosis on the roots. These should never be cut off either. Apart from this, however, it does no harm to prune back some of the roots before the potting-on is done.

Don't ever attempt to grow a plant in a larger container than is really necessary. Generally speaking, it has been found that a pot plant in the house does best when the roots are fairly close to the sides of the container. If a pot is absolutely dry when it is used, the tendency is for the earthenware to draw in much of the moisture from the compost used, and the plant roots suffer from dryness. Thus even after a pot has been sterilised and dried out, so that all the fumes disappear, it is advisable to moisten it before actual potting up takes place.

Not only does one use crocks over the whole bottom of the pot, but in cases where a largish container is used it is advisable to cover the two or three crocks with a layer of coarse peat, say an inch deep, and this will prevent the soil from trickling down between the crocks and eventually closing up the drainage hole. If by any chance the pot is to be stood outside during the summer, and this is recommended in some instances in Chapter 10, be sure not to put the pots on soil, for fear that a worm may get up into the pot. When this happens, infinite trouble takes place. Worms are excellent in the soil, but they cause far too much aeration and root disturbance in a pot.

Be sure that your potting compost is in just the right condition for use, i.e., it should be neither too dry nor too wet. A good test is to take up a handful and then close your fist. If when you open your fist again the soil remains pressed into a shape, without any water having been squeezed out of it, then you know that the compost is right. Again, when you throw the handful down on to the bench or table, it should disintegrate into individual crumbs.

The general rule about potting-on must be that in each case the potting soil be a little firmer than the compost the plant had been growing in recently. Primulas, for instance, may be started off in 60's, and the compost here is not made very firm. Then, when the plants are potted on into 48's, the compost used is made firm. The idea is to put some of the compost in the bottom of the pot over the peat, then put the ball of soil in the centre of the new pot and with a cupped hand, scoop up some of the new compost and let it trickle down around the inside of the pot, so as to surround the ball of roots. Keep moving the pot round as you do so, and keep tapping the pot on the table, so as to encourage the soil to settle down evenly.

Use, if you wish, a blunt-ended "rammer" specially shaped so that you can help to firm the new soil in the narrow space between the roots and the sides of the pot. Such a narrow rammer must be pushed in almost perpendicularly, and must be used intelligently. When the pot appears to be full and there is sufficient soil present—that is to say when you cannot press any more soil in without actually ramming hard—then there should be half an inch between the top of the soil and the rim of the pot. You must never fill a pot too full, or else you can't water it properly.

After re-potting, give the plant a really good watering and then put it in a fairly shady spot for a week or so, so that it can recover. It is bound to receive a shock during the process, and so will need your sympathy and help. It is a good thing, for instance, to syringe the plant overnight and morning. You can do this conveniently with one of the modern scent sprays filled with clean water. Never attempt to give the plant any food at this stage. It won't be able to " digest " it. After the week's or ten days' rest, the plant will probably have settled down and made new root hairs, and then it can come back to its ordinary spot and go on growing as before.

As to the soil or compost to use when potting on, the reader can get all the information necessary in Chapter 3. It is usual to start with the J.I. Potting Compost 1,* and then to pot on with J.I.P.2,* and finally to J.I.P.3.* If a plant has been growing on J.I.P.3* for a number of years, then it will be re-potted into J.I.P.3* once more. This compost is quite suitable for use as a top dressing in the case of plants that one doesn't want to pot on for one reason or another.

* See page 16.

CHAPTER 8

THE PLANT AND YOUR HOLIDAY

ONE of the problems of having pot plants is that people say to me: "What on earth am I going to do with my plants when I go on holiday." This, of course, can be a real problem for some people. There are several obvious answers (1) to dump them on your mother-in-law! or (2) to take them back to the nurseryman from whom you bought them and ask him to keep them for the time being. Fortunately there are kindly neighbours who will gladly keep an eye on your pot plants if, when they go away, you will promise to keep an eye on theirs.

Of course it very much depends on the type of pot plant that you are growing, and it equally depends on the time of year taken for your holiday. If, for instance, you are going away for winter sports, then the problem may not be so great from the point of view of watering because, as has already been said, all plants need less water in the winter than in the summer. On the other hand, there will be the increased problem of frost, because if you are leaving your house shut up completely, then it may get terribly cold. All you can do in such circumstances is to put the plants in the centre of the room, and put plenty of newspaper around them.

Don't stand the pots in a container of water because the danger in the winter is that the soil will get too sodden and cold. It is possible to stand them in a tray of damp sedge peat, especially if it can be a couple of inches deep. Having the plants on a table will be better than having them on the floor, because hot air rises and therefore the nearer they can be to the ceiling, the better!

One of the great advantages of growing Cacti and Succulents is that they need hardly any care at all. In the summer time all you will do is to give them a really good watering before you go away and then you'll place them on a table in the middle of the room so that they are away from the hot sunshine, which may pour in through the window. Such plants will be perfectly happy for three weeks without your care and attention.

With regard to the other house plants in the summer, it almost always means that you will have to enlist the help of some relation or friend. If you do this, make certain that you leave full instructions *in writing*, as to what ought to be done. Relations, and friends too, for that matter, have a habit of being over-kind, and thus over-water so thoroughly that the plants may die. Do everything you can, of course, to see that the plants are free from pests and diseases before you go away, and trim off any blooms that may be appearing. It is far better to ensure that the plant comes into flowering again when you return, than to have all the best of the blooms in evidence while you are away.

If it is impossible to get a friend to help, then something can be done, providing, you don't go away for more than a fortnight. The scheme is to enlist all the buckets or galvanised baths you have, and to fill these up with sedge peat, which you have taken care to make thoroughly wet beforehand. Put the whole of the pot in a " nest " which you prepare for it in the moistened sedge peat. The idea is that the pot should be fully surrounded with peat, but not, of course, the plant itself. Then you put the bucket containing a plant in a cool place where it will get lots of light. If you don't mind using your bath, this is often a grand place for plant storage during the holiday. The only danger is of escaping gas from a geyser. The bathroom must, however, have good windows, and it would be advisable to leave a chink of air for ventilation.

The great problem, of course, is the climbing plant which has clambered up the wall and is now growing from one picture to another. One can always encourage climbers by providing a string up which they can clamber. The thing to do with such a climber is to lift up the pot carefully and then to put it into its large bath or bucket, filled with the damp sedge peat. If the peat is sufficiently moist, then all should be well. Should the plant be in a position where it receives the direct rays of the sun from the window, erect a small screen so that it will give shade to the pot and the bucket, and prevent unnecessary evaporation. By the way, leave the door open a little if you can, so that some air can get in from another part of the house.

There is yet another alternative to the ones already given. In some cases there is a stoep, as the South Africans call it, at the back of the house, a balcony, and the plants could be placed there. If there's a sheltered spot in the garden, it would be possible to put down some coal ashes at least 1 inch deep and make a little base on which the pots could stand. (I say this because it isn't advisable, as I've told you before, to put the pot on soil for fear of worms getting in). The pots can be stood on a concrete path in the summer house, or in fact anywhere where they'll be in a certain amount of shade and shelter from the winds. Some people have told me that they don't want their neighbours coming into their houses while they are away in order to do the watering. If this is the case, be sure to stand the plants outside somewhere and then there's no difficulty.

Remember that, even if you are at home, it is quite a good thing for a plant to be outside. For instance, if you get a nice wet day in the summer, the plant will simply love it if you put it out into the open air. Some people take the trouble to put their plants out in the summer as a general rule. They don't knock them out, they just let them get all the normal sunshine and rain, and they say that they are far better as a result and live through the winter indoors much more happily. You can bury plants in the summer up to the rim of the pots in soil, so as to save watering, but if you do this, you've got to face the worm danger.

CHAPTER 9

MEDICINE AND THE POT PLANT

It would be very nice to be able to say that pot plants are never attacked by pests and diseases, but unfortunately this is not true. What it is perfectly correct to say, however, is that pot plants which are well looked after—if they are fed regularly with Liquinure, and if they are not over-watered or allowed to get too dry—do not get attacked in the same way as those poor plants which are " dragged up " instead of being " brought up " properly. A lot can be done from the point of view of hygiene. It helps if the outside of the pot is washed or scrubbed from time to time, so that no mosses or algæ can develop on it. Make certain, also, to scrape the soil at the top of the pot from time to time with the point of a small label or with one of those handy little chromium plated tools called a " widger." When mosses are allowed to cover the surface of the soil, it cannot breathe quite as it should and watering and feeding are made more difficult.

We have said that there are pests and diseases. The pests are the actual creatures like Aphides, Red Spiders, Capsids and the like. Some of them, like the green fly or black fly (Aphides) are easy to see, others like Red Spiders are so tiny that one has to look for them with a large magnifying glass and find them on the backs of the leaves together with the little whitish spiders' webbing that they will have made. Some actually tunnel into the leaves like the Leaf Miner. These tunnellings are often ribbon-like markings.

In the case of the diseases, the trouble is undoubtedly due to one of the fungi. It may be mildew, when the appearance will be a greyish-whitish dust on the leaves and stem; or rust, when it is possible to discover circular tufts of reddy brown powder on the under-surface of the leaves. Occasionally, as with roses, there is the Black Spot disease, and in this case all one finds is a round black ink-like spot on the leaf—or of course there may be a number of these spots.

It ought not to be as difficult to look after the ailments of pot plants as it is those out of doors. Indoors, one can take up a plant and examine it carefully. This can even be done under the electric light at night time, if necessary. Therefore one can see far more clearly than " grovelling " on one's hands and knees in the garden. The first thing to do, obviously, is to make certain whether the trouble is due to a disease or an insect. Look carefully for insects and do be sure to examine the under-surface of each leaf with a magnifying glass to see if there's anything there.

If the trouble is due to an insect, and particularly to Green Flies, Black Flies, Capsid Bugs, White Flies, Leaf Miners, baby Caterpillars, and Thrips, it should be possible to kill them all by fumigation. If you have a cupboard which you would guarantee was absolutely airtight, the plants can be put in there and a smoke pellet can be burnt. These Smoke pellets are usually used in a greenhouse and are one of the cheapest and quickest ways of killing pests. Tubes of 3 pellets, at the time of writing (1957), cost only 3/-. It wouldn't be safe to use one of these pellets in an ordinary room, or anywhere in the home where the fumes might leak out and affect human beings.

Therefore the better and safer method is to put one hand over the soil in the pot with the fingers carefully arranged on either side of the plant, and then to dip the foliage, stems and flowers (in the case of a flowering plant) into a solution of Liquid Derris. It helps if you first of all stir into the water one of the ordinary household detergents, say a dessertspoonful to a 2½-gallon bucket of water. Into this quantity of water a similar amount of Liquid Derris is stirred, and then the plant is immersed. The great advantage of Liquid Derris is that it is not poisonous to human beings, and so is safe to use in a normal household. Another advantage is that, when properly used, Liquid Derris will control Aphides, Caterpillars,

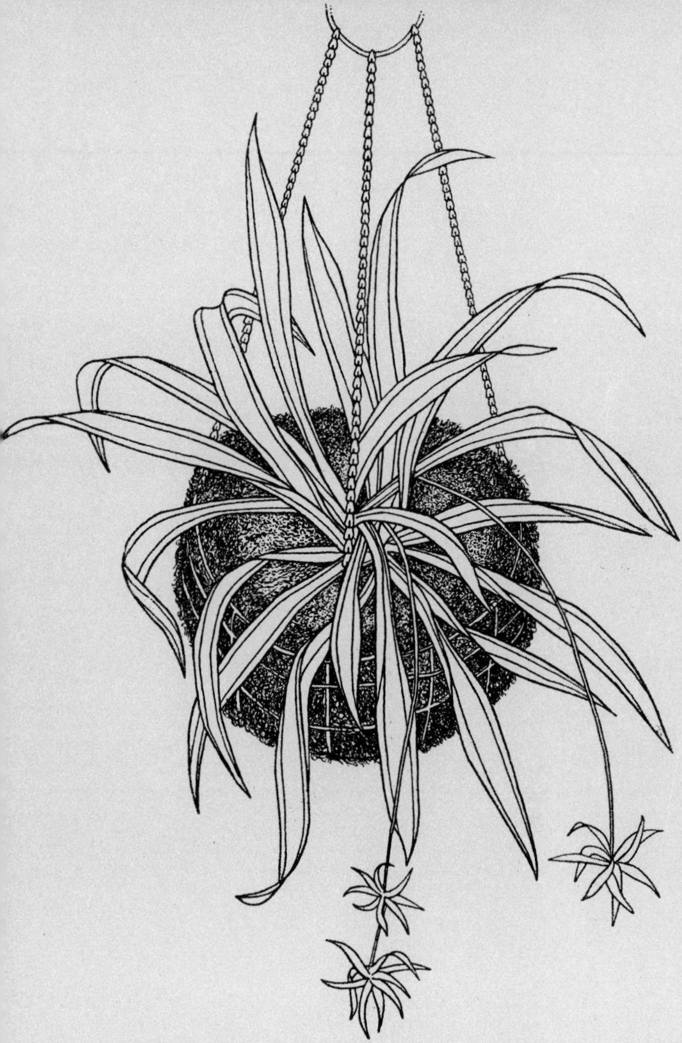

CHLOROPHYTUM ELATUM VARIEGATUM
IS EXCELLENT FOR A HANGING BASKET.

A TUBEROUS-ROOTED BEGONIA

WITH LOVELY RED AND YELLOW FLOWERS—RATHER 'BRITTLE' BUT BRILLIANT.

Thrips and Red Spiders. It will not harm the most delicate foliage and a half-pint tin (which today, 1957) costs 3/6, is the right quantity for the 2½-gallon bucket of water.

Unfortunately you will notice that the Leaf Miner is not controlled by the Derris; therefore for this it is necessary to use Liquid Nicotine,* which of course is poisonous and has to be used with care. An ounce of Liquid Nicotine is needed for a gallon of water, plus the dessertspoonfuls of detergent. A bucketful is then made up and the plant dipped in this. The alternative is to take the plant out on to the verandah or on to a path in the garden, and to give it a thorough syringing over with a nicotine wash, or " Sybol "—the Thiram wash, and do the work on a nice sunny day. You always get the best effect with nicotine when it is warm.

Sometimes Ants will invade the house in order to get on to the plants; they invariably do this in order to " milk " the Aphides (that is to say the Green Fly, Black Fly, or Blue Fly). These Aphides give out what is called honey dew, and Ants are particularly fond of this delicious beverage. Therefore, if Ants are seen always suspect the presence of Aphides. To help control the Ants, use B.H.C. dust (Benzene Hexachloride), and apply this on to the surface of the soil around the plants. The Ants will never pass this barrier. Furthermore, this dust can be used outside the house, or along the outside of the window ledge to discourage the entry of the creatures. A No. 1 sized tin is sufficient for a whole season.

There is at least one pest which may attack the roots of plants. I refer to the grubs of the Vine Weevil, which has done serious harm to Primulas and Cyclamen. If it is suspected that insect pests are actually causing trouble in the soil, the plan is to water the pots with a B.H.C. solution, and this can be bought today in shops as Sybol. A 3/6 – 4/- bottle makes 3 gallons of spray. The advantage of Sybol is that it is non-poisonous to man or even to animals or birds. It is quite easy to handle and there shouldn't be any need to add a detergent to the water when mixing it in the normal way. Be careful not to use Sybol on Hydrangeas, or on any

* Some have been successful with D.D.T.

members of the potato family, such as *Solanum capsicastrum*

Fungus Diseases

If an insect pest cannot be seen, then a fungus disease must be suspected, as has been already suggested. This may be a mildew, a rust or a black spot. For instance, on Roses you can find all three; on Chrysanthemums either rust or mildew or both; and on most other plants, either one or the other.

The best way to control the diseases is to use a fungicide based on the chemical thiram. This is now widely used and has given excellent results. It can be bought in any good horticultural chemist's as Tulisan, and fortunately it is clean to handle and easy to use. All that has to be done is to sprinkle the dispersable flakes on to water and give a good stirring. The liquid is then ready to use as a spray. The plants can be syringed thoroughly and no deposit will be left on the foliage or flowers. If by any chance it should be necessary use an insecticide, as well as a fungicide at the same time, then readers will be glad to know that Tulisan can be mixed with Sybol so as to give simultaneous control of an insect pest and a fungus disease.

Brief Description of Pests

Aphides or Plant Lice. You may have come across Green Fly, which are perhaps the most commonly encountered members of this family, but which only form a small part of it. There are Black Aphides, Mealy Aphides on roots and many others. They are usually found to start with on the undersides of leaves and, unless dealt with quickly, multiply rapidly. They are small sucking insects.

Capsid Bug. When small the Capsid Bug is yellow, but soon turns to a greenish colour. It is sometimes confused with Green Fly, but the latter are slow moving, while the Capsids are usually very active.

Leaf Miners. Sometimes you will find on the leaves of some plants a sort of mosaic work. If this is closely examined it will be found that it is a little tunnel through the centre of the leaf and the Leaf Miner, which makes the tunnel, will be found at the end of it.

Red Spiders. These are not so much little spiders as little mites. Sometimes the foliage will turn a peculiar brown colour and if it is examined a sort of whitish webbing will be found underneath. If you look at this through a magnifying glass little yellow or red mites will be found.

Thrips. These are tiny little insects, being only about one twentieth to one thirtieth of an inch in length. They are drab in colour and long and narrow in shape. Where they feed on the leaves little white areas will be seen, surrounded by little black dots, their excreta. If a sheet of white paper is held below the affected leaf and then the leaf is tapped, some of the thrips may drop on to the piece of paper and thereby be recognised.

Vine Weevil. These are black and about a third of an inch long. The black is minutely specked with yellow. They are like little beetles and their usual custom is to nibble at the edges of the leaves, leaving little scalloped marks.

CHAPTER 10

FLOWERING POT PLANTS

THOSE who know my books will realise that I always try to deal with plants in a methodical manner. Furthermore, the species and varieties included are those which are known normally to be successful. I have no room for the "miffy" little plants which have to be tended and coddled in order to make them grow and flower. Give me a good robust plant that is really happy to live and consequently makes me happy.

In this Chapter, then, there will be found a list of the flowering pot plants which can be grown in the house at normal room temperatures without any extra special trouble and attention. Care has been taken in each case to give a brief description of the plant and to say what time of the year it flowers. Please note also that the headings are the same in the case of each plant—thus we always find that Time of Flowering comes first, then Propagation, next Position, then Temperature, and so on.

I do hope that this carefully compiled list of plants will prove to be of value to those who are going to grow flowering pot plants in the days to come.

In Chapter 11 will be found a list of the flowering pot plants suitable for use as hanging plants. Some will plant them in hanging baskets, some will use them in pots in windows, and others will purposely put them on ledges where they can look their best cascading down.

ABUTILON

(Flowering Maple)

An erect and semi-climbing shrub, which is valuable for its fine foliage as well as for its drooping bell-shaped flowers.

Time of flowering: Spring and early summer.

Propagation: (1) Cuttings early spring or summer on bottom heat of 65 deg. F.

(2) Seeds sown in January or February.

Position: Sunny, can be put out in garden in summer.

Temperature: Cool during winter months.

Feeding: Liquid manure once a week when plants are established and growing well.

General Management: Re-pot in March. Water freely in spring and summer, moderately in autumn and winter. Grow in J.I.P.3.

General Remarks: Young plants are to be preferred.

Pruning: In February prune hard.

ABUTILON MEGAPOTAMICUM

Species cultivated:

A. hybridum: Most of the Abutilons commonly grown are hybrids, with flowers of various colours—yellow, red, orange and white.

A. megapotamicum (Syn. *A. vexillarium*) has yellow and red flowers and is often used as a hanging plant.

AGAPANTHUS

(African Lily)

Blue or white tubular flowers on stems about three feet long. Leaves are long, narrow and fleshy.

Time of flowering: May and June.

Propagation: Should be divided in spring as growth commences.

Position: Large pots or tubs in the sun.

Temperature: March to September 45 to 55 deg. F.
September to March 32 to 40 deg. F.

Feeding: Can be fed frequently during growing period with liquid manure.

General Management: They dislike root disturbance and

grow better when pot-bound, so should only be re-potted when really necessary. Water well during growing season, but give less in winter. Can go outside in summer.

General Remarks: These plants grow to a good size, so are best for larger rooms.

Species cultivated:

A. umbellatus, bright blue var. *albus* is white.

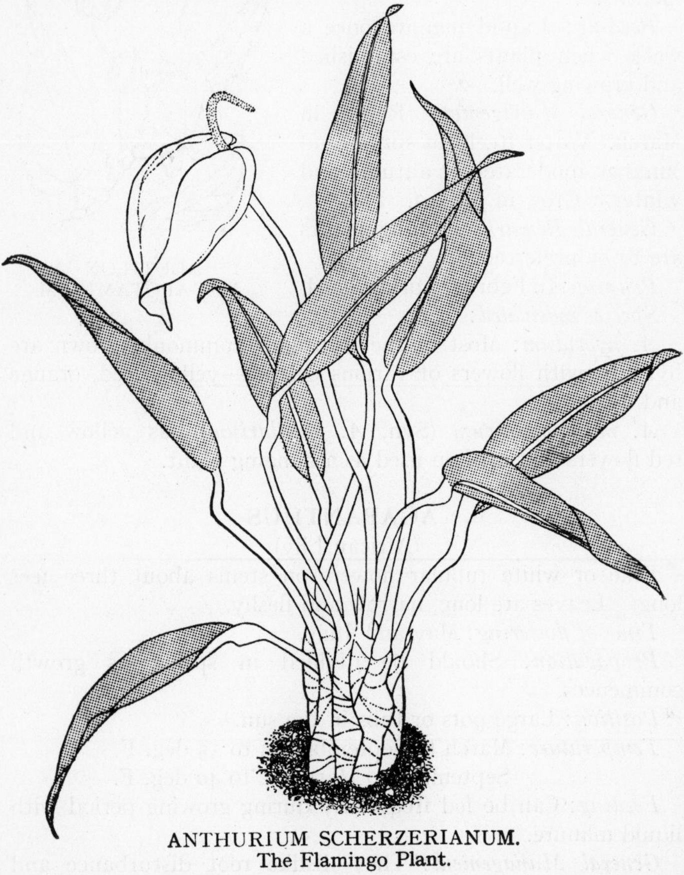

ANTHURIUM SCHERZERIANUM.
The Flamingo Plant.

ANTHURIUM

(Flamingo Plant)

Plants with ornamental foliage and brightly coloured flowers on long stems. The flowers are flat with a spathe in the centre.

Time of flowering: March to August.

Propagation: (1) Division of roots in March.

(2) Ripe seeds sown in spring in sandy compost. Keep moist at temperature 80 deg. F.

Position: Semi-shade away from bright sunlight.

Temperature: Cooler in winter, but should not drop below 55 deg. F.

General Management: Re-pot in March with good drainage. Water freely in spring and summer. Prefers moist conditions and moss can be grown round base of plant. J.I.P.3.

General Remarks: This is not an easy plant to grow, but well repays trouble by its spectacular colour.

Species cultivated:

A. Scherzerianum: Leaves widely ovate—lanceolate with deep-red flowers.

Var. *Rothschildianum* has red spathes spotted with white.

A. crystallinum has ornamental longer leaves with white veins.

APHELANDRA

An evergreen flowering shrub, the flowers being surrounded by beautifully-coloured bracts.

Time of flowering: Autumn and winter.

Propagation: (1) By seeds when obtainable.

(2) By cuttings of half-ripened wood or young growth in March or April on bottom heat.

Position: Not usually permanent house plants and when not indoors should be kept in warm greenhouse.

Temperature: March to September 70 to 80 deg. F.
September to March 60 to 65 deg. F.

General Management: Water in summer and keep atmosphere moist. Keep drier in winter. Re-pot in March in J.I.P.3. Prune shoots to within an inch of base in February.

Species cultivated:

A. squarrosa, with yellow flowers and orange-yellow bracts.

A. squarrosa, Louisia, beautiful leaves and exotic yellow plume-like flower.

ARDISIA

(Spear Flower)

Evergreen shrubby plant, covered with red berries in autumn and winter.

Time of flowering: June.

Propagation: (1) By seeds early spring over bottom heat 75 deg. F.

(2) By cuttings of half-ripe wood in March at same temperature.

Position: Semi-shade.

Temperature: Hardy in summer, but must not be frosted in winter.

General Management: Re-pot in February or March in J.I.P.3. Water freely in summer but sparingly in winter.

General Remarks: They make useful room plants during the winter months when thickly covered with berries.

Pruning: Cut back in March.

Species cultivated:

A. crispa (Syn. *A. crenata* or *crenulata*).

ASTILBE

An herbaceous plant useful for potting up in autumn and bringing into the house. Red, pink and white flowers in spikes.

Propagation: Division in autumn.

Position: Sunny.

Temperature: Average.

General Management: Pot up in J.I.P.3 in autumn. Can go back into garden again in spring. Keep leaves and roots moist.

AZALEA

Most of the Azaleas grown as house plants are either varieties of the species *Azalea indica* (Indian Azalea) or varieties of the

Kurume Azalea. They are evergreen shrubs with white, pink, mauve or scarlet flowers.

Propagation: (1) Indian Azaleas are usually grafted in spring, but cuttings may be taken of half-ripened shoots in July and August.

(2) Kurume Azaleas can be propagated in the same way as *Azalea indica*, but can also be layered in the spring.

Position: Pots in the sun during winter months, but can be put out in partial shade during the summer.

Temperature: Warm to bring into bloom.

Feeding: Weekly with liquid manure after buds have formed.

General Management: Keep well-watered, if possible with rain water containing no lime. Re-pot every two years after flowering in J.I.P.3. Keep lime out of compost.

General Remarks: Foliage should be syringed if the atmosphere is dry, but syringing should stop when the flowers are coming into bloom. Pick off seeds after flowering and syringe to produce buds for next season.

Species cultivated:

A. indica. Many varieties including the following:

Blushing Bride, blush pink.
Niobe, a double ivory white.
Max Shame, pink with white frill.
Schryveriana, double rose edged with white.

Kurume hybrids:

Hatsugiri, lilac.
Hinodegiri, bright crimson.

BEGONIAS

As flowering plants Begonias can be divided into the tuberous and fibrous-rooted sections. Certain rhizomatous-rooted Begonias, such as Begonia Rex are grown for their foliage. The tuberous Begonias are usually the more popular of the types, and the flowers in some cases may be huge. There are single or double varieties, frilled varieties, in various shades of pink, red, orange, yellow and white.

Tuberous Begonias

Propagation: (1) Cuttings of young shoots in spring and early summer.

(2) Seeds sown in a temperature of 65 to 75 deg. from February to April.

Position: Not in direct sunlight.

Time of flowering: Summer and autumn.

Temperature: Warm during growing season, but cooler in winter.

Feeding: When in full growth feed weekly.

General Management: The tubers are started into growth in February and March by planting in boxes in a mixture of peat and sand. As soon as the tubers are rooted, pot them up. To obtain good size blooms later on, it is best to pick the early flowers off. Keep well watered during the growing period. After flowering has ceased and the growth dies down in the autumn, water should be witheld. The pots can be stored on their sides during the winter.

General Remarks: Very useful plants, which go on for years if the tubers are kept. As the stems are brittle and the flowers weighty, it may be necessary to stake. The larger tubers can be divided, provided that there is a shoot to each segment.

Fibrous-rooted Begonias

Time of flowering: Autumn, winter and early spring.

Propagation: (1) Leaf cuttings in spring and summer.

(2) Shoot cuttings in February or March.

Position: Not in direct sunlight.

Temperature: About 55 deg. in winter.

Feeding: Occasional feeding during growing season.

General Management: Water carefully, but keep rather dry after flowering until March. Grow in J.I.P.3 and re-pot when necessary in March.

General Remarks: Where the atmosphere becomes dry through central heating, the leaves should be sprayed from time to time. The flowering period should be quite long provided that they are kept reasonably cool.

Species cultivated:

B. coccinea has scarlet flowers and spotted leaves.

B. fuchsioides has scarlet flowers and green leaves.

B. Gloire de Lorraine (var. of *B. cheimanthus*) has bright pink flowers and is perhaps the best known fibrous-rooted Begonia.

B. Scharffiana has leaves which are green on top and red underneath. The flowers are white.

B. glaucophylla has brick-red flowers and can be used as a hanging plant.

BILLBERGIA

Evergreen plants with showy flowers and leaves in rosettes and clusters.

Time of flowering: Spring.

Propagation: Rooted side-shoots can be potted up in April in a temperature of 85 deg. F.

Temperature: Warm during winter months, hot during summer.

General Management: Water well but do not let it get too wet, otherwise rotting may occur. They prefer a light position, but not direct sunlight. Use J.I.P.3.

General Remarks: They prefer a moist warm atmosphere and can be fed fairly frequently with liquid manure.

Species cultivated:

B. nutans has yellowish green flowers with blue margins. Bright red bracts.

B. zebrina has prickly-toothed leaves, spotted and banded with white. The flowers are yellowish green.

BILLBERGIA NUTANS.

BOUVARDIA

A dwarf evergreen shrub with fragrant flowers.

Time of flowering: September to December.

Propagation: (1) Cuttings of young shoots 2 or 3 ins. long in March in temperature of 65 deg. F.

(2) Root cuttings about two inches long in spring, but results are rather erratic from this method.

Position: Sunny position, especially in summer.

Temperature: Preferably about 55 deg. F. in winter.

Feeding: Feed with liquid manure weekly from September to June.

General Management: Re-pot at end of March using J.I.P.2. Can be watered moderately in spring, freely in summer, and just kept moist in winter.

General Remarks: They can be hardened off from June to September in a cold frame. These plants are not very easy to keep owing to their requirements of a moist warm atmosphere.

Pruning: About the end of February prune hard back leaving only about one inch of the previous year's growth.

Species cultivated:

Varieties and hybrids are commonly cultivated with red, yellow, white and pink flowers.

BROWALLIA

An herbaceous plant, often grown as an annual, but which makes a good pot plant. Blue, violet or white tubular flowers.

Time of flowering: Depending on time of sowing.

Time of sowing: Seeds sown in spring will flower in late summer and seeds sown in July will flower over the winter.

Position: Half-shade.

Temperature: Fairly warm.

Feeding: Feed once or twice weekly when the plants fill the pots and the flower buds appear.

General Management: The plants need pinching back two or three times to encourage bushy growth. The plants from the July sowing may be grown in a cold frame until the end of September. When brought indoors, they should be syringed frequently. Finish in J.I.P.3.

Species cultivated:

B. elata (Syn. *B. americana*) has blue or white flowers.

B. speciosa major has large bright blue flowers with white throats.

BRUNFELSIA

An evergreen flowering shrub with large scented flowers.

Time of flowering: Mainly in autumn and winter.

Propagation: Cuttings of ripened wood from new growth either in spring or autumn at temperature of 65 deg. F.

Position: In the light, but not in the direct sunlight.

Temperature: Hot in summer and warm in winter.

Feeding: Feed once a week during the summer months with liquid manure.

General Management: Water freely in the summer but only moderately in the winter. Syringe in spring and summer.

General Remarks: These shrubs flower best when pot-bound, so do not pot on unless really necessary. Grow in J.I.P.2.

Pruning: Thin lightly after flowering. Pinch back young shoots when about six inches long so as to get bushy plants.

Species cultivated:

B. calycina (Syn. *Franciscea calycina*) has purple fragrant flowers. The variety *eximia* has rich purple flowers fading to almost white.

CALCEOLARIA

(Slipper-flower or Slipperwort)

Valuable pot plants growing from one to three feet high, with large, bright-coloured flowers sometimes blotched and spotted. They can be divided into the herbaceous species and the shrubby species.

Harbaceous Species

Time of flowering: May to October.

Propagation: By seeds sown in July.

Position: Semi-shade.

Temperature: Cool.

Feeding: Feed once a week from April until the plants come into flower.

General Management: Young plants should be potted up as soon as they are large enough to handle and then whenever required. Over winter the plants should be watered moderately, but the pots should not be allowed to dry out. They can be watered freely after April. Use J.I.P.2.

General Remarks: It is essential to have cool conditions throughout for growing Calceolarias. The seed germinates at a low temperature and they prefer a cool shady corner to grow in. Discard after flowering.

Species cultivated:

There are many species and varieties of herbaceous Calceolarias cultivated.

Shrubby Species

Time of flowering: Summer.

Propagation: (1) By cuttings in spring.

(2) By seeds sown in March at a temperature of 50 to 60 deg. F.

Position: Out of strong sunlight.

Temperature: Cool conditions.

Feeding: Feed established plants once a week.

General Management: Young plants should be potted on as required and should be pinched back to promote bushy growth. They should be re-potted in March and cut back into shape. Can go outside in summer.

General Remarks: The soil should be kept moist, but not sodden.

Species cultivated:

C. integrifolia (Syn. *C. rugosa*) yellow to red-brown flowers, not spotted.

C. mexicana has pale yellow flowers.

CALLISTEMON

(Bottle-brush tree)

An evergreen shrub with leathery leaves and dense spikes of flowers like bottle-brushes.

Time of flowering: June.

Propagation: Cuttings three inches long in August under a bell-glass in a temperature of 55 to 65 deg. F.

Position: In the sun. Good ventilation.

Temperature: Coolish.

General Management: As the plants prefer to be pot-bound, they should only be re-potted every two or three years in March or April. They may be watered freely in summer, but only moderately in winter, never allowing the roots to dry out however.

General Remarks: They are very suitable for room plants and are not difficult to keep going. The foliage should be syringed during hot weather. They should be grown in J.I.P.2, but in the years when they are not being re-potted they can be top-dressed. They can be fed with liquid manure during the summer months.

Species cultivated:

C. lanceolatus (Syn. *C. citrinus. Metrosideros floribunda. M. semperflorens. M. citrina*) is the species usually grown with bright red flowers.

CAMELLIA

An evergreen flowering shrub, which can be used as a house plant when small.

Time of flowering: Early spring.

Propagation: (1) Cuttings of firm shoots in July.

(2) Layering in September.

(3) Grafting in March (difficult).

(4) Seeds sown in March in temperature of 75 deg. F.

(5) Leaf cuttings with heel in summer.

Position: Full sun and can go out in summer in sunny spot.

Temperature: Cool over winter.

Feeding: Feed over winter once a week.

General Management: Should be re-potted in August every two or three years. Use J.I.P.1 as they do not like a rich soil. The plants should be kept moist before the buds come out and the foliage should be sprayed.

General Remarks: These are difficult plants, which should, however, repay the trouble taken. Keep out of draughts and do not let the roots dry out.

Pruning: Once the plants are trained very little pruning is necessary and that should be done in March.

Species cultivated:

C. japonica. Nearly all the cultivated varieties are of this species. There are a number of different varieties, amongst which Princess Bacchoiochi, imbricated, red, and *Chandleri elegans*, pink, semi-double, might be mentioned.

CHRYSANTHEMUM

One of the few varieties of Chrysanthemum which can be considered solely as a pot plant is the variety "Charm." In the autumn there is a mass of small flowers in the usual Chrysanthemum colours.

Time of flowering: Autumn.

Propagation: Seeds sown in March with slight bottom heat.

Position: In sun. Can be outside during the summer.

Temperature: Cool.

Feeding: Feed once a week with liquid manure when established.

General Management: Pot on, finishing up in 7 in. pots and J.I.P.3.

General Remarks: The variety "Charm" is not stopped or disbudded. It is best discarded after flowering and new plants grown from seed. It is possible, however, to retain a very good plant and take cuttings from it.

CINERARIA

A well-known pot plant with large leaves and numerous daisy-like flowers ranging from white, through pink and red to mauve and blue. They are usually grown as annuals.

Time of flowering: From Christmas to April.

Propagation: By seeds sown in April to July in a temperature of 65 to 75 deg. F.

Position: In sun. Usually placed in summer in cool shaded frame.

Temperature: Cool. Objects to hot dry conditions.

Feeding: Feed twice a week with diluted Liquinure from September onwards.

THE CINERARIA.

A plant for Christmas and the New Year, needs plenty of water.

General: Pot up seedlings when large enough and then pot on as required. Finish in 5 or 6 in. pots using J.I.P.2.

General Remarks: They definitely do like cool conditions. It is probably best to buy the plant when it is ready to flower, and discard it after flowering. Careful watering is necessary.

Species cultivated:

C. cruenta (Syn. Senecio cruentus) is the parent of the hybrids now grown. The smaller varieties make the most suitable room plants.

CLIVIA

(Kaffir Lily)

Fleshy-rooted plants, with dark, long, narrow, evergreen leaves. The showy flowers are in shades of scarlet, orange and yellow, 15 or 20 in a cluster, on stems about 2 feet high.

Time of flowering: December to July.

Propagation: (1) Division of roots when re-potting.

(2) Seeds sown in March at temperature of 75 deg. F. The seeds must be absolutely ripe.

Position: Prefers the sun, but will support a shadier position.

Temperature: Cool over winter.

Feeding: When established can be fed with liquid manure once a week.

General Management: The plants can be put out in the summer and watered freely. Moderate watering during winter months. They prefer being pot-bound and dislike being transplanted, but when re-potting is absolutely necessary it should be carried out in February.

General Remarks: The plants like plenty of food and moisture. J.I.P.3 should be used.

Species cultivated:

C. miniata, scarlet and yellow. There are a number of varieties of *C. miniata* which are superior to the species and also many good hybrids.

COFFEA

(Coffee Tree)

Useful for its dark glossy green foliage and for its small flowers followed by scarlet berries in the autumn.

Time of flowering: September. Berries in autumn.

Propagation (1) By sowing ripe, fresh beans over bottom heat.

(2) By ripe cuttings inserted in sand with bottom heat. A bell-glass should be used.

Position: In the light, but not in the direct sunlight.

Temperature: Warm.

General Management: Should be re-potted several times a year using J.I.P.3. Water can be given freely.

General Remarks: It is probably best for these plants to be raised in a hot greenhouse, but they should do well afterwards in warm, well-ventilated rooms, with plenty of light.

Pruning: Little required and let them grow on their own.

Species cultivated:

C. arabica (Arabian Coffee). Small white flowers in clusters of four or five.

CROSSANDRA

A dwarf evergreen shrub with orange-scarlet flowers.

Propagation: By cuttings of shoots 2 to 3 ins. long at almost any time in a temperature of 85 deg. F.

Time of flowering: March.

Position: In the light with good ventilation.

Temperature: Hot in the summer, warm in the winter.

General Management: Re-pot in March using J.I.P.2 and giving good drainage. Water well in summer, but more moderately in winter.

General Remarks: This is not one of the easiest plants to grow, but provided that it is given good ventilation and plenty of space, i.e. not surrounded by other plants, it should do well. It is possible to keep it flowering for a good portion of the year.

Species cultivated:

C. infundibuliformis (Syn. *C. undulifolia*).

CRYPTANTHUS

A dwarf, often stemless plant with greenish-white flowers.

The flowers appear in a mass in the middle of the leaf head. For treatment see *Billbergia*.

Species cultivated:

C. zonatus.

CYCLAMEN

(Sowbread)

Well-known perennial flowering plant. The leaves are often marbled and marked and the flowers are white, or various shades of pink, crimson, cerise or salmon-scarlet.

Time of flowering: Winter.

Propagation: Seeds sown ¼ in. deep from August to November, or January to March in a temperature of 55 deg. F.

Position: In the sun. Can go outside in dry, shady spot in summer.

Temperature: Moderate.

Feeding: Feed once a week with liquid manure when in flower.

General Management: Re-pot in July or August using J.I.P.1. The corm should always be partly above the surface of the soil. After re-potting water moderately and syringe until the new growth begins, then water freely until the plants have ceased to flower. Keep almost dry from May to July.

General Remarks: They make good room plants, which can be kept from year to year, but which are often discarded after flowering. One year old seedling plants are probably the best. Lime may be left out of the potting compost as they are not lime tolerant. Can be watered from underneath, which will ensure that no water lies in the top of the corm, thereby causing it to rot.

Species cultivated:

C. persicum is the parent of most of the numerous hybrids and varieties which can be purchased.

CYTISUS

(Broom)

One species is commonly grown in pots. It makes a small compact bush and produces freely bunches of small, fragrant, yellow, pea-like flowers.

Time of flowering: Spring and early summer.

Propagation: (1) Heel cuttings in March or August of young shoots 2 to 3 ins. long in temperature of 75 to 85 deg. F.

(2) Seeds sown in March in temperature of 65 to 75 deg. F. Seedlings do not always come true to type, but probably produce the best plants.

Position: In full sun. Can be put out in the garden from July to October.

Temperature: Cool from October to February, but then warmer until flowering time.

Feeding: Once a week when the plants are in flower.

General Management: Re-pot in May or June using J.I.P.2. Water during flowering season when necessary, but don't over-water. At other times water moderately. Syringe in hot weather.

General Remarks: The plants should be pinched back in order to produce bushy growth. They like plenty of air and do not like heat.

Pruning: Prune well back after flowering.

Species cultivated:

C. x racemosus (Syn. *Genista formosa*) is usually grown. Also *Cytisus fragrans*, see page 2.

ERANTHEMUM

These plants are grown for their ornamental foliage as well as for their flowers.

Time of flowering: Early spring.

Propagation: Cuttings root easily in spring in temperature of 75 deg. F.

Position: In the sun, especially for the variegated leafed varieties. In the summer they can be put in a cold frame.

Temperature: Should have warmth in the spring.

Feeding: Feed from time to time during flowering period.

General Management: Re-pot in March or April when necessary, but do not over-pot. Use J.I.P.3. Water moderately in winter and freely at other times.

General Remarks: They should be kept well-pruned back in order to form a tidy plant. As they tend to get straggly with age, it is best to propagate new plants from time to time.

Species cultivated:

E. pulchellum (Syn. *E. nervosum* and *Daedalacanthus nervosus*) has dark blue flowers and glabrous leaves.

E. Wattii (Syn. *Daedalacanthus Wattii*) has deep purple flowers.

ERICA

(Heath)

Small evergreen shrubby plants, with white, mauve and pink flowers. They may be divided into two groups, the hard-wooded kinds, which are difficult to propagate and the soft-wooded kinds, which are easier to grow, but not so easy to keep alive.

Time of flowering: December to August.

Propagation: Cuttings early in the year and in mid-summer at a temperature of 60 to 70 deg. F.

Position: In the sun when established. Can be outside from July to October.

Temperature: Cool.

Feeding: Feed occasionally with weak liquid manure during the summer.

General Management: Heaths in common with other members of the *Ericaceae* are lime-haters. They should be watered, if possible, with rain water. They prefer a peaty, sandy compost but will grow in J.I.P.1 and should be re-potted after flowering.

General Remarks: Heaths are not easy plants to keep from one year to the other.

Pruning: This should take place immediately after flowering and should be fairly drastic with the soft-wooded variety. The hard-wooded varieties need little pruning, except that the dead flowers should be removed.

Species cultivated:

Hard-wooded kinds:

E. x Cavendishiana has rich yellow flowers from May to July.

E. ventricosa and varieties. Flowers June to August.

Soft-wooded kinds:

E. hyemalis is a popular South African heath and has rosy-white flowers in winter.

There are many soft-wooded species and varieties grown.

EUPHORBIA*

Flowering shrubs with ornamental leaves, but usually known for their bright scarlet bracts. *E. pulcherrima* (Poinsettia) needs quite different methods of cultivation from the other two species often grown, i.e., *E. fulgens* and *E. splendens* Crown of Thorns), therefore it is being mentioned separately for convenience.

Time of flowering: Summer to winter.

Propagation: Cuttings from old wood taken during summer months. Wood should be stopped from bleeding by dipping in fine sand or charcoal.

Position: Warm room with plenty of light and moisture.

Temperature: Warmth, but not heat throughout year.

General Management: Should be watered with warm water when necessary, but be careful not to overwater. Use J.I.P.3† and feed well when established.

General Remarks: These plants are not very easy to keep in the average room, as they demand moister conditions than are usually offered. If they can be given these conditions, such as by surrounding the pots with moist sedge peat, it should be possible to keep them going satisfactorily. In most cases, however, it will probably be advisable to buy the plants ready for flowering and discard them when the flowering is over.

Euphorbias: Culture for *E. fulgens* and *E. splendens.*

Time of flowering: Summer to winter.

Propagation: By cuttings, which should be sealed off with charcoal or sand and left to dry for about two weeks before insertion. Propagation is then easy.

Position: Sunny. Can go in the garden during the summer.

Temperature: Warm, but not hot.

General Management: These plants are quite easy to manage and should be potted in J.I.P.3. Do not over-water as they are best kept on the dry side.

General Remarks: These plants are best in a dry atmosphere.

* Euphorbias have been included under Flowering Plants, although it is, of course, realised that they might be included under Foliage Plants, as the crimson bracts for which they are noted are modified leaf scales.

† See page 18

Care should be taken not to get the milky juice from these plants on to the skin, as in a number of cases it is poisonous.

FRANCOA
(Bridal Wreath)

Grows two to three feet high, while flowers in dense spikes.

Time of flowering: July and August.

Propagation: (1) Division of plants at potting time.

(2) Cuttings of shoots in summer.

(3) Seeds sown under bell-glass in temperature of 50 to 55 deg. F. in February, March or April.

Position: Does well either in the sun or shade.

Temperature: Cool during winter and put out in garden in summer.

General Management: Keep well potted as it likes plenty of room, using J.I.P.3.* It is better to renew the plants every three or four years. Well-rooted plants can be fed once or twice a week.

General Remarks: They do well as room plants and can be propagated fairly easily.

Species cultivated:

F. ramosa.

FUCHSIA
(Lady's Ear-Drops)

An attractive flowering shrub which is easy to grow and maintain.

Time of flowering: Summer.

Propagation: (1) Cuttings of young shoots from January to March in temperature of 70 to 80 deg. F. From April to September the cuttings can be taken in a cool house or indoors.

(2) Seeds sown in March or April in a temperature of 55 deg. F.

Position: Likes light but does not want to be in sunny window. In winter keep in cool frost-free place.

Temperature: Cool.

Feeding: Feed once a week when plants are well established.

General Management: Re-pot in spring using J.I.P.3. Keep

* See page 18

well watered in summer but dry off in winter, not allowing them, however, to become dust-dry. Young plants should be kept well pinched back in order to promote bushy growth.

General Remarks: They can be put out in the garden in the summer. Fuchsias are easy to propagate at home and generally are no trouble at all, if not allowed to dry out while flowering.

Pruning: With old plants cut well back in spring to encourage fresh growth.

Species cultivated:

There are numerous hybrids and varieties suitable for growing in pots.

GARDENIA

Evergreen shrubs with fragrant white flowers.

Time of flowering: Spring and summer.

Propagation: (1) By cuttings of semi-ripe shoots over winter in temperature of 70 deg. F.

(2) By layering.

Position: Not in the bright sunlight.

Temperature: Hot in the summer and warm in winter.

Feeding: Feed occasionally when plants are in flower.

General Management: Re-pot in March using J.I.P.2. Should be sprayed frequently during hot weather and can be watered freely in summer, more sparingly in winter. Use rain water if possible as they are lime-haters.

General Remarks: They are not easy plants to look after and need quite a lot of attention. It is probably advisable to buy them in the first place rather than propagate them.

Species cultivated:

Gardenia jasminoides (The Cape Jasmine) has fragrant white flowers in summer and there are a number of worthwhile named varieties.

GLOXINIA

(*Sinningia speciosa*)

Tuberous plants with large, bell-shaped flowers of various colours. The leaves are large and hairy.

Time of flowering: Summer and early autumn.

Propagation: (1) Cuttings of shoots 1 to 2 ins. long inserted in small pots under a bell-glass in a temperature of 65 to 75 deg. F. (2) Cuttings of leaves in a temperature of 55 to 75 deg. F. (3) Seeds sown in March in a temperature of 65 to 75 deg. F.

Position: Not in the full sun.

Temperature: Hot during growing season, warm during dormant period.

Feeding: Once a week after flower buds have appeared.

General Management: The tubers should be potted up singly in small pots, and should be potted-on as soon as they have started into growth. The tuber should not be quite buried and should be firm in the pot. Water should be given sparingly at first and then more freely, but the plants should not be over-watered. After flowering the pots should be dried out gradually and kept dry until the spring.

General Remarks: Attempts should only be made to raise these plants where there is a greenhouse, as they are not easy subjects. As room plants they only have a short flowering period, but their velvet-like flowers in various colours are very attractive.

Species cultivated:

Sinningia speciosa is the Gloxinia and there are numerous varieties. The flowers can be spotted or plain and the colours range from scarlet and white to lilac and purple.

HYDRANGEA

Deciduous shrubby plants with large heads of flowers.

Time of flowering: Spring and summer.

Propagation: Cuttings taken in March or April in a temperature of about 60 deg. F., or by ripe cuttings taken in August with no heat.

Position: Plenty of sun.

Temperature: Cool.

Feeding: Feed once a week when the plants are growing vigorously.

General Management: Re-pot in February or March using J.I.P.2. Water freely in summer but keep drier in winter. Pink varieties may be tinged blue, by adding one of the proprietary blueing chemicals to the water when watering a month or two before the plant is due to come into bloom. White varieties cannot be treated. Use rain water, if possible, as the plants are lime-haters.

General Remarks: Sun helps to bring out the colour in the flowers, but once they are in bloom they will last longer if they are put in a shadier spot. Some of the bought Hydrangeas are not easy to keep as they are often over-forced. It is not advisable to bring them into the warmth too early in order to induce flowering.

Species cultivated:

H. Macrophylla var. *Hortensia* is the common Hydrangea and is the one usually grown in pots.

H. paniculata grandiflora is usually grown outside, but can be grown in pots.

IMPATIENS

(Balsam)

Quick-growing, soft-stemmed plants with brightly coloured flowers.

Time of flowering: Summer and autumn.

Propagation: By seed sown from March until May in a temperature of 60 deg. F.

Position: In the light, but not too much sun.

Temperature: Warm.

General Management: They can be quite easily grown from seed. They must be potted on as soon as necessary as they require plenty of room and are very quick-growing. Plenty of water can always be given. J.I.P.3 can be used for the final potting and the plants can be fed two or three times a week when the roots have filled the pots. Plants should be discarded after flowering.

General Remarks: They are not difficult to grow provided that there are facilities for raising any plants from seed.

Species cultivated:

I. Balsamina. There is both a rose and a camellia flowered strain. Colours range from white, mauve, violet to salmon-pink and scarlet.

I. Sultanii. (Busy Lizzie) Shades of pink and red, single.

IXORA

(West Indian Jasmine)

A small evergreen shrub with clusters of fragrant flowers.

Time of flowering: Summer.

Propagation: Cuttings from two or three inches long in a temperature of 75 to 85 deg. F. taken from March to May.

Position: Good light but not in direct sunlight.

Temperature: Hot in summer and warm in winter.

Feeding: Feed once or twice a week when plants are in flower.

General Management: Re-pot in February or March using J.I.P.1. Water freely except after flowering, when they can be dried out a bit. Syringe frequently in spring and summer.

General Remarks: These plants are difficult to propagate, but when once they are established they can be kept for years. They love heat and moisture and hate draughts, especially during the flowering period.

Species cultivated:

I. fulgens has clear scarlet and orange flowers becoming scarlet.

JACOBINIA

Perennial plants with pink, nettle-like flowers.

Time of flowering: Summer and winter.

Propagation: Cuttings of young shoots from March to July in a temperature of 75 deg. F.

Position: Is better in partial shade. Can be put out in garden in summer.

Temperature: Fairly cool in winter.

Feeding: Can be fed twice a week when in flower.

General Management: Re-pot in March or April. Water freely in summer but more sparingly in winter. Pinch back young plants to encourage bushy growth.

General Remarks: This can be very successful as a house plant, acclimatising itself quite easily to indoor conditions. It should have plenty of ventilation and should never be allowed to dry out.

Pruning: Prune hard after flowering.

Species cultivated:

J. carnea has flesh-coloured flowers in August and September.

J. coccinea has scarlet flowers.

MALVASTRUM

(False Mallow)

Small shrubby plant with numerous purple flowers.

Time of flowering: Practically continuous.

Propagation: (1) By seeds.

(2) By half-ripe cuttings in the spring with slight bottom heat.

Position: In the sun, but cool conditions over winter.

Feeding: Feed once a week during the summer.

General Management: Pot in J.I.P.3 and water well in summer months, but more sparingly in winter. Re-pot fairly frequently and have good drainage.

General Remarks: They can be propagated quite easily and make good house plants. Should be discarded after every three years and put out in the garden during the summer.

Species cultivated:

Malvastrum capense. Purple flowers.

M. hypomadarum. Pinky-white flowers with purple streaks.

MARGUERITE

(*Chrysanthemum frutescens*)

A useful flowering plant for pots, with its small white daisy-like flowers.

Time of flowering: Summer.

Propagation: By cuttings taken in April (this can be done in the home).

Position: Out of doors during the summer. Likes bright conditions.

Temperature: Moderate during winter months.

Feeding: Well-established plants can be fed once a week.

General Management: Once the cuttings are rooted, they can be potted up singly and potted-on as required. J.I.P.2 can be used. They can be pinched back two or three times in order to promote bushy growth. Water can be given freely during the growing period.

General Remarks: It is probably advisable to discard tne plant after it has flowered, except where greenhouse space is available or it is desired to keep a stock plant for future propagation.

NERIUM

(Oleander, Rose Bay)

Evergreen shrubs with brightly coloured flowers, which are fragrant in some varieties.

Time of flowering: Summer.

Propagation: By cuttings of mature shoots 3 to 6 inches long in spring or summer in a temperature of 60 to 70 deg. F. Sometimes they can be rooted in water.

Position: In the sun. Can be put outside during the summer.

Temperature: Cool.

Feeding: Feed once or twice a week during the summer.

General Management: Re-pot in February or March using J.I.P.2. The roots should fill the pots, which should be large. Water copiously during the summer, when the roots can be waterlogged, but keep almost dry in the winter. Watering should be carried out with rain water, if possible, as they are not lime-tolerant.

Pruning: Shorten back shoots after flowering, but care should be taken as flowers are formed on previous year's shoots.

General Remarks: These plants are poisonous if eaten and should be kept out of the reach of children.

Species cultivated:

Nerium oleander is the common oleander with rosy flowers. but there are a number of varieties with flowers in a range of colours such as rose, red, purple and yellow.

OXALIS

(Wood Sorrel)

Tuberous-rooted plants with clover-shaped leaves and various coloured flowers. It is possible by the selection of suitable species to have plants in flower most of the year round.

Time of flowering: Mostly spring and summer.

Propagation: (1) Division of roots at potting time.

(2) Offsets at potting time.

(3) Seeds sown in spring at a temperature of 55 to 65 deg. F.

Temperature: Cool.

Position: Light, but not too much sun.

Feeding: Feed established plants occasionally with liquid manure.

General Management: Spring-flowering species should be planted in January or February, and summer-flowering species in March or April. The roots should be planted ½ inch deep, watered sparingly until the leaves start to grow, and then freely. After flowering watering should be reduced gradually until the leaves have quite died down, then the plants should be kept dry until time for re-potting.

General Remarks: They make useful house plants and their culture is not difficult.

Species cultivated:

O. enneaphylla has bluish-white flowers in June.

O. rosea has rose-pink flowers in spring.

O. rubra has darker pink flowers in spring.

PELARGONIUM

There are two main types which are grown in pots and are much used as house plants. The Show Pelargonium and the Zonal Pelargonium, the latter being commonly called Geranium. Ivy-leafed Pelargoniums are more suitable as hanging plants.

Show Pelargoniums

Time of flowering: Spring and early summer.

Propagation: Cuttings of firm shoots two to three inches long in July or August, no heat required.

Position: In the sun.

Temperature: Moderate.

Feeding: Well-rooted plants can be fed twice a week until the flowers open.

General Management: Pot on rooted cuttings firmly as they require it and pinch back to promote bushy growth. Old plants may be re-potted in August or September, but it is not

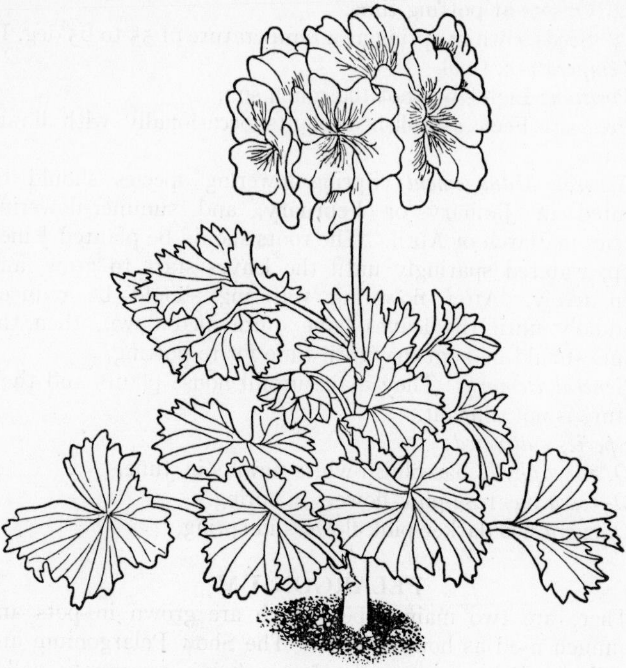

A SHOW PELARGONIUM
with interesting leaves and flowers.

worth keeping them more than two years. Water freely from March to June, but sparingly at other times. Cut back shoots to within one inch of their base in July.

General Remarks: They are old-fashioned plants but still may be considered some of the best room plants. They are no trouble to maintain and can be raised easily in the house. Do not over-water.

Species cultivated:

P. domesticum is the Show Pelargonium and there are numerous varieties readily available with blotched or plain coloured flowers, in various shades of pink, red and white. Regal Pelargoniums have semi-double flowers.

Zonal Pelargoniums or Geranium

Time of flowering: Can be timed to flower either in winter or summer.

Propagation: For summer flowering by cuttings of shoots in August or September; for winter flowering by cuttings in February and March. If cuttings are very sappy in August or September they can be withered in the sun for 24 hours. No hormone rooting chemicals need be used.

Position: In the sun. Can be put out in the summer. Winter flowering plants may also be put out in a warm, sheltered position from June to September.

Temperature: Moderate. Winter flowering plants need more heat during the winter than the others.

Feeding: The plants can be fed twice a week when well-established.

General Management: Pot on rooted cuttings firmly when necessary, using J.I.P.2. Pinch back young plants to promote bushy growth. Little water required at any time and good drainage essential.

General Remarks: Although old plants can be kept from year to year, it is probably best, as propagation is so easy, to grow a batch of new plants every year. Avoid frost at any cost.

Species cultivated:

There are many varieties of the Zonal Pelargonium, in various shades of pink, red and white flowers, some single, some semi-double.

In addition there are many varieties of ornamental and coloured foliage Geraniums, as well as scented-leaved Geraniums. Their culture is the same as for the Zonal Pelargonium.

PRIMULA

These are well-known plants with single or double flowers in heads. Some of the species have hairy leaves.

Time of flowering: Winter and spring.

Propagation: (1) By seeds sown in March, April or May. (2) By division in some species, such as *P. obconica*.

Position: Shade, but give more light during winter.

PRIMULA SINENSIS.
A delightful small flowering pot plant

Temperature: Moderate.

Feeding: Feed occasionally before flowering, but overfeeding causes too much green growth.

General Management: Young plants should be potted on as soon as they require it, but not too firmly. Pot fairly deeply with some of the leaves resting on the soil, this will give the plants better anchorage, as new roots will spring out from the stem. Give plenty of air and keep the soil moist. Do not over-water or the leaves will quickly turn yellow.

General Remarks: Unless facilities for propagation are available it is probably best to purchase the plants when they are coming into bloom. Species other than *P. malacoides* are often kept from year to year, but young plants are usually the best. Some varieties of *P. obconica* may need 6-in. pots, but 5-in. pots should be sufficient for the others.

Species grown:

P. malacoides has smaller leaves and flowers than the other species. The flowers are usually coloured pale lilac, but pink, rose and white varieties may be obtained.

P. obconica is perhaps the most common species grown, with large flowers in pink and mauve shades. The leaves of this plant are hairy and affect the skin of some people, causing an irritating eczema.

P. sinensis has large flowers with frilled petals and may be obtained in pink, white, deep-rose, scarlet, crimson and bluish mauve.

P. Kewensis is a hybrid with yellow flowers.

There are many other species and varieties of Primula.

REINWARDTIA

(Yellow Flax)

A small sub-shrub with yellow flowers.

Time of flowering: Winter and spring.

Propagation: By seed or cuttings on slight bottom heat in March.

Position: In the sun, but will appreciate shade in summer, when it can go outside.

Temperature: Moderate.

Feeding: Can be fed with liquid manure during growing season.

General Management: Pot in J.I.P.2. Prefers cool, well-ventilated atmosphere.

General Remarks: It is best to discard older plants.

Pruning: Keep well pruned back to promote bushy growth.

Species cultivated:

R. indica (Syn. *R. trigyna* and *Linum trigynum*) is the Yellow Flax.

RUELLIA

(Christmas Pride)

Small flowering shrubs with funnel-shaped flowers.

Time of flowering: Winter

Propagation: By cuttings in spring or summer in temperature of 75 to 85 deg. F.

Position: Shady conditions, except in winter when it can be placed in sunny window.

Temperature: Warm in winter.

General Management: Re-pot in February or March. Should be watered freely in spring and summer, but more sparingly at other times. Use J.I.P.2.

General Remarks: Syringe the foliage frequently. As it gets unsightly after flowering, buy in new plants.

Pruning: When young frequent pruning should keep the plant in shape.

Species cultivated:

R. macrantha rosy-purple.

SAINTPAULIA

(The African Violet)

A very popular perennial for the house, with fleshy, hairy leaves and flowers ranging from white to deep-violet.

Time of flowering: Mainly from March to August, but can be made to flower at other times.

Propagation: (1) By leaf cuttings at any time of the year, with about an inch of the stem in the rooting medium. They can also be rooted in water.

(2) By seed sown in spring in a temperature of 65 to 70 deg. F.

(*Note*: It is not easy to propagate these plants in the home.)

Position: Never in the direct sun.

Temperature: Moderate, but warmer in winter if required to flower then.

Feeding: Feed occasionally during growing season.

General Management: Re-pot in J.I.P.2 in February or March. Watering should always be done from underneath, as overhead watering tends to rot the plant. They like warmth and do not care for draughts. Do not spray.

General Remarks: They make very good house plants as they need little light. A test to see whether they have enough light can be made by putting a hand between the plant and the nearest source of light. If a shadow is cast on the plant then the light is sufficient. Although they can be kept from year to year, it is probably more satisfactory to buy in new plants as they are coming into bloom.

Species cultivated:

S. ionantha has many cultivated varieties.

SOLANUM

(The Winter Cherry)

The small, well-known shrub with orange-red berries at Christmas time.

Time of flowering: Insignificant flowers in summer, berries in winter.

Propagation: By seeds sown in February over bottom heat of 65 deg. F.

Position: In the light. Can be put in garden in summer.

Temperature: Cool.

Feeding: Can be fed during growing season with balanced liquid manure.

General Management: Final potting should be in J.I.P.2 using 48's. Keep well pinched back to promote bushy growth.

General Remarks: These plants can well be kept for a second year if they are cut back to half their size and put out in a warm sunny place in the garden. They should not be over-watered, but on the other hand should not be allowed to dry out. They can be kept drier after they have been pruned and until they have been put out of doors. They should not be put next to Tomatoes, which are of the same family and have similar diseases.

Species cultivated:

Solanum capsicastrum flowers like those of the potato with red berries like cherries to follow.

STREPTOCARPUS

(Cape Primrose)

Large tubular flowers of many shades, pink, blue, violet, red, rosy-purple and white, are produced two or three together on stout stems.

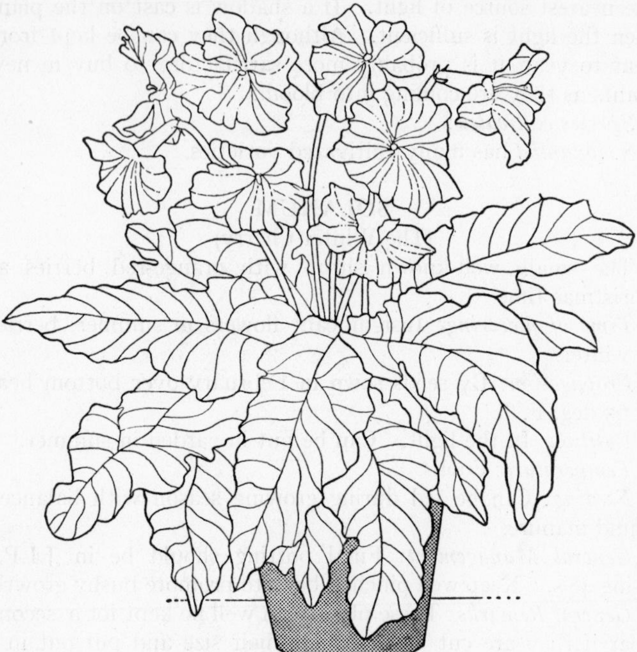

STREPTOCARPUS HYBRIDUS.
An unusual flowering plant for the summer.

Time of flowering: Summer.

Propagation: (1) Division of plants in March.

(2) Leaf cuttings in summer.

(3) Seeds sown in temperature of 55 to 65 deg. F. in February, March or April.

Position: Half-shade.

Temperature: Moderate, does not like hot conditions.

Feeding: Feed once a week when plant is well established.

General Management: Seedlings should be potted on as required, but not too firmly. Old plants may be re-potted in March in J.I.P.3. Water freely in summer, but keep almost dry in winter. Give plenty of space.

General Remarks: These plants are usually propagated by a nurseryman and discarded after flowering. They are often used with other pot plants to give colour.

Species cultivated

S. hybridus. There are numerous hybrids of the various species which are most commonly cultivated.

TILLANDSIA

Curious perennial plants with leaves in rosettes and coloured rosettes.

Cultivation: As for Billbergias.

Species cultivated:

T. Lindeniana has bluish-purple flowers in large spikes with carmine bracts.

VIBURNUM TINUS

This species of Viburnum with its small pink flowers can be used as quite an attractive pot plant.

Time of flowering: Winter months.

Propagation: By half-ripe cuttings in spring or ripe cuttings in August on bottom heat.

Position: Likes light, but not strong sunlight.

Temperature: Cool.

General Management: Re-pot every two or three years in J.I.P.2. In order to stop excessive growth may be root-pruned.

General Remarks: Feed occasionally during summer with liquid manure. Keep moist but do not over-water.

Species cultivated:

V. Tinus (Syn. *Laurestinus*) has numerous horticultural varieties.

VRIESIA

Perennial plants of the *Bromeliaceae* similar to Tillandisa.

Cultivation and Propagation: As for Billbergia.

Species cultivated:

V. speciosa (Syn. *V. splendens*, *V. picta*, *V. zebrina*) has leaves with dark brown bands and yellowish-white flowers, with dark red bracts. The variety Major is a more robust form.

ZANTEDESCHIA (Richardia)

(The Arum, Calla Lily, Lily of the Nile)

This is the well-known Arum Lily. There is also a species with yellow flowers in addition to the white.

Time of flowering: Winter, spring and early summer.

Propagation: (1) Division of plants in August and September.

(2) Offsets in August or September.

(3) Seeds sown in spring in temperature of 65 to 75 deg. F. (It takes three years to get a flowering plant from seed.)

Position: In the light, but not in direct sunlight. Can be put outside from June to September, with pots laid on side.

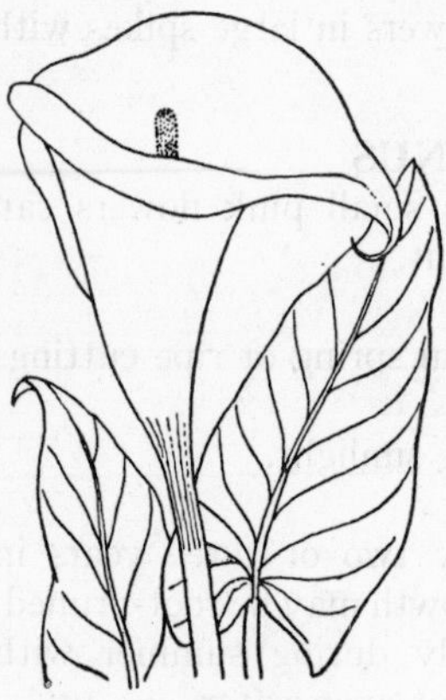

ZANTEDESCHIA AETHIOPICA

Temperature: Cool.

Feeding: Feed once a week when pots are filled with roots.

General Management: Large pots will be needed. Use J.I.P.2 and re-pot in August. Shake old soil from roots and pot up in fresh compost. Cut any damaged piece of tubers away and dust cut ends with lime or charcoal. Keep roots moist during growing season, but dry off after flowering and store pots on their sides.

General Remarks: They prefer to be watered from underneath, so place pot in saucer. During the growing season they do not mind being waterlogged.

Species cultivated:

Z. aethiopica (Syn. *Richardia aethiopica* and *africana*). The Common Calla has white flowers growing about 2½ ft. high. Many varieties.

Z. Elliottiana is The Golden Calla and has bright green leaves spotted with white.

CHAPTER 11

FLOWERING POT PLANTS SUITABLE FOR USE AS HANGING PLANTS

IN this Chapter is given a list of those flowering pot plants which are considered especially suitable for use in hanging baskets, either in windows or on walls.

CAMPANULA

Although this genus is usually cultivated in the open, there is one species, *C. isophylla,* which makes a useful hanging house plant. The flowers are lilac or lavender-blue or white.

Time of flowering: June or July and throughout summer.

Propagation: (1) Basal cuttings in heat.

(2) Seeds sown in temperature of 55 to 65 deg. F.

Position: In baskets in the sun. When not flowering can be more in the shade and can go outside in the summer.

Temperature: Cool.

Feeding: Feed once a week with liquid manure when the flower spikes begin to show.

General Management: Re-pot, if necessary, in March. Plants can be watered freely in summer and moderately in winter. Use J.I.P.3.

General Remarks: Prefer cool conditions. To prolong the flowering, dead flowers should be cut off.

COLUMNEA

Pretty evergreen trailing shrub. Flowers scarlet and yellow.

Propagation: Cuttings of firm shoots about 3 ins. long in February in temperature of 85 deg. F.

Position: In hanging baskets; not in strong sunlight.

Temperature: Warm

General Management: Plant in March, water freely in summer, moderately in winter. Can be fed once a week with liquid manure during the summer.

General Remarks: These are not easy plants to grow.

Species cultivated: *C. gloriosa* and *C. Banksii*.

EPISCIA

Small plants with hairy leaves, tinged with copper or red.

Time of flowering: Spring and summer.

Propagation: (1) By cuttings in the spring. (2) By division.

Position: Like the shade. They can support light but should never be in full sun. Prefer wire baskets.

Temperature: Warm.

Feeding: Can be fed once a week when growing strongly with liquid manure.

General Management: Plant in March, water freely in summer and moderately in winter. Use J.I.P.2.

General Remarks: These are not the easiest of plants to grow, but are well worth a try. Discard plants after they have flowered, unless a greenhouse is available.

Species cultivated:

E. cupreata is the most common species. Flowers scarlet.

JASMINUM

(Jessamine or Jasmine)

The species *J. Mesnyi* (Syn. *J. primulinum*) with its flat, yellow flowers is very suitable for growing in hanging baskets.

Time of flowering: Winter.

Propagation: (1) Cuttings of firm shoots from March to September under a bell-glass in a temperature of 65 to 75 deg. F. (2) Heel cuttings in spring at a lower temperature.

Position: In hanging baskets in the sun.

Temperature: Warm, but not hot.

General Management: Pot or plant in February or March using J.I.P.2. Water freely in spring and summer, more moderately at other times. Keep atmosphere moist.

General Remarks: Do not over-pot and give them plenty of air. They can be placed outside in the summer months. provided that there is a warm corner available.

LINARIA CYMBALARIA (Syn. *Cymbalaria muralis*)
(The Wall Ivy)

A small trailing plant with blue flowers, yellow at the throat.

Time of flowering: Most of year.

Propagation: (1) Seed in spring.

(2) Splitting the long stems, and pegging down in soil.

Position: They prefer shady and moist conditions, although flowering is encouraged by more light. Can go outside.

Temperature: Cool.

General Management: Is easily grown. Pot in J.I.P.2. Water freely, but do not keep too wet in winter.

General Remarks: These were common greenhouse plants and can be propagated very easily. Keep in small pots.

Species cultivated:

L. Cymbalaria. Varieties include alba with white flowers, maxima with large flowers and rosea with pink flowers.

LOTUS

Small shrubby plant with silvery leaves and small scarlet flowers.

Time of flowering: Late spring.

Propagation: (1) Cuttings of shoots in summer at temperature of 55 to 65 deg. F. (Cuttings root easily).

(2) Seeds sown in March or April with bottom heat.

Position: In a hanging basket in good light.

Temperature: Cool.

Feeding: Feed plants once a week when in flower.

General Management: Re-pot in February or March using J.I. Seed Compost. Plenty of ventilation can be given when weather is suitable. Water moderately in summer and very sparingly in winter.

General Remarks: Can be put out in the garden in summer. As it is easily grown from cuttings, it makes quite a suitable house plant to raise indoors. The plants should be replaced when they get ugly and out of shape.

Species cultivated:

L. Berthelotii (Syn. *L. peliorhynchus*). The variety *atro-coccineus* has darker red flowers spotted with black.

LYSIMACHIA

The species *Nummularia,* commonly known as Creeping Jennie or Charley, can be used as a hanging or basket plant. It has small round leaves and yellow flowers.

Time of flowering: Summer.

Propagation: By division.

Position: In a basket or on the wall in the shade.

Temperature: Cool.

General Management: Re-pot in J.I.P.2 when necessary and keep moist. Do not over-pot.

General Remarks: This is an easy little plant to grow and is quite happy as long as it is kept moist.

Species cultivated:

L. nummularia. The variety aurea has yellow foliage.

PELARGONIUM

(Geranium)

The Ivy Geranium (*P. peltatum*) makes a very useful hanging plant. It is best in a sunny position. Colours range from deep-rose to white.

General Cultivation: See Zonal Pelargonium.

SPIRONEMA

A Mexican plant with large leaves; fragrant white flowers.

Propagation: By cuttings. These root easily.

Position: Hanging plant in the half shade.

Feeding: Feed occasionally with liquid manure.

Temperature: Warm.

General Management: Re-pot when necessary using J.I.P.2. Water freely in summer, but more carefully in winter.

General Remarks: This plant can be put out in the garden in the summer, but likes warmth during the winter months.

Species cultivated:

S. fragrans has white fragrant flowers on older plants.

TROPAEOLUM

(Nasturtium)

This is the common Nasturtium of the garden.

Time of flowering: Summer.

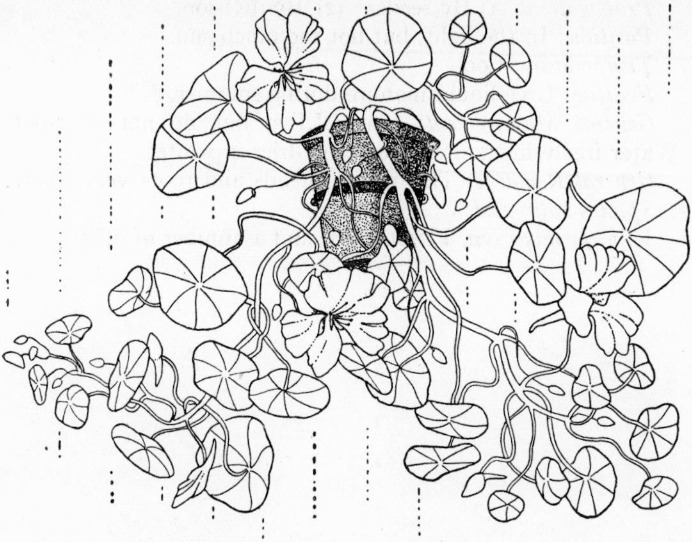

A TROPÆOLUM in a wall pot screwed to the wall.
You may call it a Nasturtium!

Propagation: By seeds sown in spring.

Position: In the sun.

Temperature: Warm.

General Management: Pot in J.I.P.1. Do not over-water. Use rain water, if possible.

General Remarks: They make excellent hanging plants for the house. Plants should be discarded after flowering.

Species cultivated:

T. majus (Garden Nasturtium) has a number of varieties.

T. minus (Dwarf Nasturtium), with smaller flowers.

VERONICA

(Speedwell)

The mass of pale blue flowers in the spring, and the small oval leaves, make this a very useful hanging plant.

Time of flowering: Spring.

Propagation: (1) By seeds. (2) By division.

Position: In the light, but not too much sun.

Temperature: Cool.

Feeding: Give liquid manure during summer.

General Management: Use J.I.P.3, but do not over-pot. Water freely in summer, but keep drier in winter.

General Remarks: This plant spreads and roots very easily.

Species cultivated:

V. filiformis (Syn. *V. filicaulis*) and a number of others.

CHAPTER 12

FOLIAGE POT PLANTS

In this chapter will be found pot plants, which are *normally* grown more for their foliage than for their flowers. They are more often difficult to grow and look after, and all of them have their devotees in this country. Read through the lists carefully and see which you prefer. Take special notice of the *General Remarks* please.

ALBIZZIA

A small mimosa-like tree with graceful foliage. Pale yellow flowers in spring.

Propagation: By seeds. Can be raised indoors. Sow in spring.

Position: Moderate sun. Can go out in garden in summer.

Temperature: Moderate.

Feeding: Feed well during growing period.

General Management: Pot in J.I.P.2 using medium-sized pots. Can be watered well during maximum growth.

General Remarks: They make good room plants. As they are easy to raise from seed, it is probably better to grow new plants every season. Old plants tend to get leggy.

Species cultivated: *A. lophantha.*

ARALIA (see **Fatsia**)

ARAUCARIA

One of the few small conifers suitable for growing indoors.

Propagation: (1) Sow ripe seeds in temperature of 65 deg. F. (2) Soft wood cuttings in autumn.

Position: Although it prefers a sunny position, it can put up with considerable shade.

Feeding: Occasional.

General Management: Grow in J.I.P.1. Do not over-pot and only re-pot occasionally as the roots are better not disturbed.

General Remarks: This is quite an easy room plant and was much more commonly grown than it is now. It is slow-growing. Can be put out in the garden during the summer.

Species cultivated:

A. excelsa is the Norfolk Island Pine.

ASPARAGUS

Ornamental plants with fern-like foliage.

Propagation: (1) Division of roots in March.

(2) Seeds sown in spring in temperature of 65 deg. F.

Position: Partial shade. Airy conditions.

Temperature: Moderate.

Feeding: Well-established plants may be fed weekly.

General Management: Re-pot old plants in March using J.I.P.2. Young plants should be potted-on as necessary. Water freely during summer, giving less in winter, though the roots should always have ample. Syringe frequently during the summer if possible.

General Remarks: These are well-known room plants and should give no trouble. They are easy to propagate.

Species cultivated:

A. plumosus is the Asparagus Fern and has delicate fern-like shoots. It can be used as a climber. The variety *nanus* is perhaps the most commonly grown and makes a good dwarf plant.

A. Sprengeri has long drooping shoots and sharp spines. The small whitish flowers are followed by red berries. There are a number of varieties. This species is often used for hanging baskets.

ASPIDISTRA

(Parlour Palm)

An evergreen plant with large, wide leaves and insignificant flowers just above the soil surface.

Propagation: Division of roots during summer.

Position: Not in strong sunlight.

Temperature: Cool.

General Management: These plants will thrive for years in the same pots, but re-potting when it has to be done should be carried out in March. Water freely in summer, but more moderately in winter. Use J.I.P.1.

General Remarks: These plants were very much more popular than they are now. Their culture is extremely easy and they can live to a good age. If a variegated variety produces a green leaf, it should be cut off at once, otherwise it may grow at the expense of the variegated ones.

Species cultivated:

A. lurida is the most widely grown. The variety *variegata* has leaves with alternate stripes of green and white.

AUCUBA

The well-known evergreen shrub, with insignificant flowers followed by scarlet berries.

Propagation: By cuttings during winter over slight bottom heat.

Position: In the half-shade. Outside during the summer.

Temperature: Moderate.

General Management: Pot in J.I.P.2 and ensure good drainage.

General Remarks: The leaves can stand up to considerable dust and smoke, but are better for a syringing or sponging occasionally. There are male and female plants. The female plant will not produce berries unless fertilised by the male. Fertilisation can be done by hand with pollen kept from the male plant. The pollen keeps its vitality for some weeks.

Pruning: Early pruning will help to keep a good shape.

Species cultivated:

A. japonica has a number of cultivated varieties. The variety *variegata* is the well-known spotted one and is usually male. Var. *nana* is dwarf and compact, and bears berries.

There are numerous other varieties of *A. japonica*.

BEGONIA

The Begonia Rex hybrids are well known foliage plants, having variegated leaves in a considerable range of colours. The flowers are insignificant, compared to the leaves.

Propagation: (1) By seeds sown in January to February in a temperature of 65 to 75 deg. F.

(2) By leaf cuttings in spring and summer.

(3) By shoot and stem cuttings in spring.

(Propagation in the home is not advised.)

Position: In the light but shaded from the sun.

Temperature: Moderate.

General Management: Re-pot in March using J.I.P.3 and

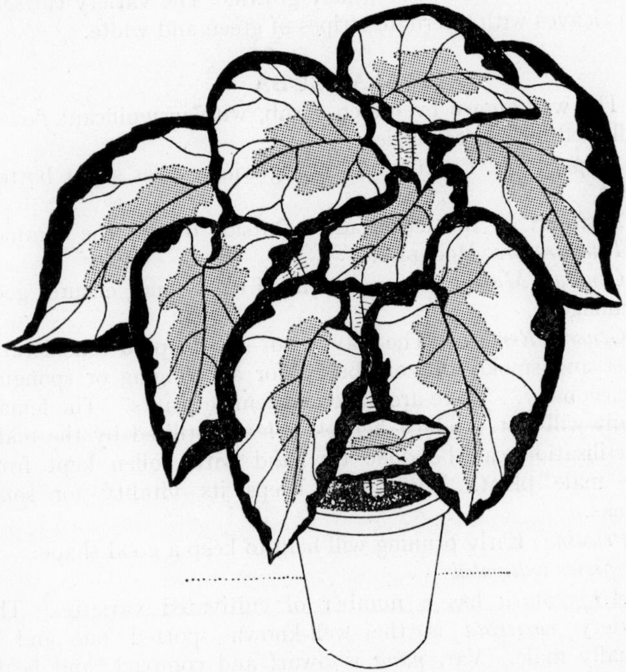

BEGONIA REX.

A Begonia grown for its charmingly coloured leaves.

largish pots. Water fairly freely in summer, but more moderately in winter. Feed every few days with liquid manure during the growing season.

General Remarks: These are very useful foliage plants. In winter it is advisable not to get the leaves too wet, as rot may be caused; a soft brush may be used for cleaning the leaves. On the other hand they do like a moist atmosphere and are not fond of central heating. Again they are not suitable for places which are very dusty owing to the difficulty of cleaning the leaves.

Species cultivated:

Begonia Rex hybrids have green leaves covered with mixtures of red, pink and grey. The flowers are pink.

B. ricinifolia has large bronzy-green leaves and pink flowers. It can grow more in the shade and is less trouble than the Begonia Rex hybrids.

CAREX

A perennial plant with ornamental grass-like foliage.

Propagation: By division of roots of established plants in March.

Position: Can support shade.

Temperature: Cool.

General Management: Do not over-pot, but re-pot in March when necessary. Water freely during the summer and never let the pot dry out. Water moderately during the winter months, otherwise the roots may rot. They make quite handsome house plants.

Species cultivated:

C. Morrowii variegata (Syn. *C. japonica* and *C. tristachya*) has stiff, long-pointed leaves, with a white line near the margins.

CHLOROPHYTUM

Evergreen perennials with striped grass-like leaves. Small white, insignificant flowers.

Propagation: (1) By splitting in spring.

(2) By cuttings in spring.

(3) By runners.

Position: In light or shade, but leaves develop brighter colours in the light.

Temperature: Moderate.

Feeding: Feed with liquid manure once a week when established.

General Management: Pot in J.I.P.2 leaving plenty of room at top of pot. Water freely in summer and more sparingly in winter, but never over-water.

General Remarks: They make very useful hanging plants when older, as little plantlets form after the flowers have faded, thereby weighing down the stems. It can easily be propagated in the home. If the plant fills up the watering space at the top of the pot, then watering will have to be done from underneath by means of a saucer.

Species cultivated:

C. Comosum has white-striped leaves. Var. *picturatum* has yellow-striped leaves.

C. elatum variegatum has longitudinal white lines on the leaves.

CITRUS

(Orange)

A small evergreen shrub with white fragrant flowers and large orange fruits.

Time of Flowering: Summer.

Propagation: (1) By cuttings in July.

(2) By seed. Plants can easily be raised from seed indoors, but they will not always flower.

Position: In full sun. Can go out in sheltered spot in summer.

Temperature: Cool.

Feeding: Feed once a week during summer months.

General Management: Pot in J.I.P.2, using large pots and giving good drainage. Re-pot when necessary in spring. Water freely in spring and summer, moderately in winter. Syringe daily in summer.

General Remarks: Orange trees are, as a rule, easy to grow. They should always be kept in shape, and cut well back to promote bushy growth. As they are usually grown more for their evergreen foliage effect than for their flowers, they have been included in this chapter.

Species cultivated:

C. aurantium is the Seville or Bitter Orange.

C. sinensis is the Sweet Orange.

CODIAEUM

(Croton or South Sea Laurel)

Shrubby, evergreen plants, with leaves beautifully marked in red, yellow, mauve and green shades.

Propagation: (1) Cuttings of shoots at any time in a temperature of 75 deg. F.

(2) Stem-rooting in March or April.

Position: Full sun will produce the best colours in the leaves, but will grow in the shade.

Temperature: Hot in summer and warm in winter.

General Management: Re-pot in March using J.I.P.2, but keep in as small pots as possible. Water freely in summer, moderately at other times.

General Remarks: The plants are not easy to grow and keep without a hothouse being available. They are very pretty, however, during their short life indoors. Avoid draughts and feed once a week with liquid manure. Syringe well to create a moist atmosphere and avoid trouble with red spider.

Species cultivated:

C. variegatum pictum (or *C. hybridum*) is the Croton.

COLEUS

(Flame Nettle or Nettle Geranium)

Ornamental plant with bright and variously coloured nettle-shaped leaves. Usually grown as an annual.

Propagation: (1) By cuttings of young shoots whenever available.

(2) Seeds sown in February at a temperature of 75 deg. F.

Position: Good light brings out the best colours.

Temperature: Hot in summer, warm in winter.

Feeding: Feed once a week with liquid manure when established.

General Management: Young plants should be potted-on as required and pinched back frequently in order to promote bushy growth. Water freely during summer and moderately at other times. Old plants should be re-potted in February or March using J.I.P.2.

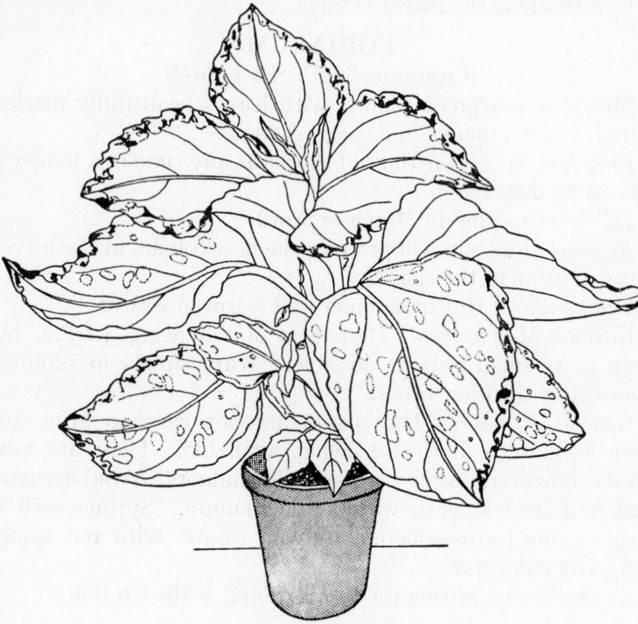

COLEUS.

A plant grown for its gorgeous leaves—usually propagated each season.

General Remarks: These plants are really best when grown as annuals. It is probably easiest to buy a good young plant from a florist and discard it when it has passed its best, unless a greenhouse is available.

Species cultivated:

C. Blumei has yellow, dull red or purple leaves. The variety *Verschaffeltei* has purplish-red leaves. There are many varieties of this species.

CORDYLINE

Evergreen foliage plants with long leaves, striped in various colours.

Propagation: (1) Seeds sown early in year on bottom heat.

(2) Stem rooting in March or April.

(3) Offsets at any time.

Position: In the light, but not direct sunlight. Outside in summer.

Temperature: Cool over winter.

General Management: Keep in as small pots as possible giving good drainage. Use J.I.P.2. Water well in summer, but more moderately in winter, keeping fairly dry to give rest.

General Remarks: They are very useful as they are reasonably hardy, even though they prefer warm conditions. Plenty of air should be given.

New plants can easily be propagated from stem cuttings.

Species cultivated:

C. australis has narrow leaves. There are numerous varieties with leaves in varying colours.

C. indivisa has wider leaves with red or yellow midribs.

(Cordylines in the past have often been listed as Dracaenas.)

CYANOTIS

A small cushion plant with different shaped leaves.

Propagation: (1) By cuttings taken at almost any period.

(2) By division.

Position: In the bright sun, but can have more shade in winter.

Temperature: Warm.

General Management: Pot in J.I.P.2, using plenty of drainage in pot. Water freely during growing period, but otherwise moderately.

General Remarks: This is quite an easy little plant to propagate and grow. It is related to the Tradescantia.

Species cultivated:

C. barbata has narrow leaves and dark blue flowers.

C. somaliensis has hairy leaves.

A simple, but most effective plant.

THE CORDYLINE.

CYPERUS

(The Umbrella Plant)

Ornamental plants with grass-like foliage and elegant flat flowering heads with greenish-brown flowers.

Propagation: (1) By division of roots in March or April.

(2) By cuttings or heads of flowers with a small piece of stem attached.

(3) By seeds sown early in year in temperature of 55 to 60 deg. F.

Position: In partial shade.

Temperature: Warm in summer and cool in winter.

General Management: Pot in J.I.P.3, but keep under-potted if anything. Can be copiously watered from underneath,

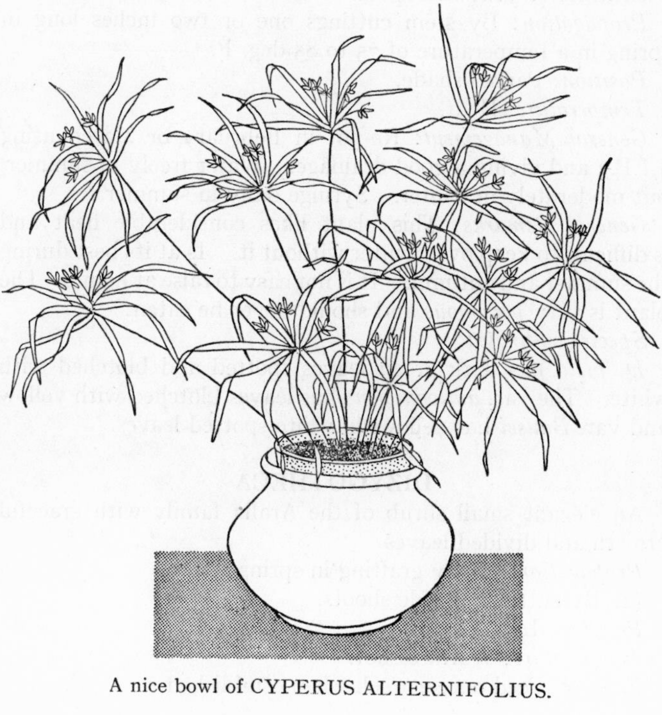

A nice bowl of CYPERUS ALTERNIFOLIUS.

leaving water in the underpot or saucer. Feed once a week when well established.

General Remarks: These are very good plants for the house and go well in bowls. They are easy to propagate and very little trouble to look after.

Species cultivated:

C. alternifolius has long, narrow leaves and var. *gracilis* even narrower leaves.

C. diffusus has wider leaves and greenish-brown spikelets.

DIEFFENBACHIA

(Dumb Cane)

A shrubby plant with oblong leaves, sometimes marked with white or yellowish spots.

Propagation: By stem cuttings one or two inches long in spring in a temperature of 75 to 85 deg. F.

Position: Partial shade.

Temperature: Heat.

General Management: Re-pot in February or March using J.I.P.3 and giving a good drainage. Water freely in summer, but moderately in winter. Syringe daily in summer.

General Remarks: This plant likes considerable heat and is difficult to keep over winter without it. Is at its best during the summer and autumn. It is not easy to raise at home. The plant is very *poisonous* and should never be eaten.

Species cultivated:

D. picta has dark green leaves spotted and blotched with white. The var. *antioquiensis* has leaves blotched with yellow and var. *Bausei* has yellowish, white-spotted leaves.

DIZYGOTHECA

An elegant small shrub of the Aralia family with graceful growth and divided leaves.

Propagation: (1) By grafting in spring.

(2) By cuttings of side shoots.

Position: In the light.

Temperature: Warm to hot.

Feeding: Feed once a week when established.

A DIEFFENBACHIA.

A good window plant for a town house—
needs partial shade.

General Management: Re-pot in March in J.I.P.2, giving plenty of drainage. Do not over-pot. Water well in summer, but give rest by watering moderately in winter.

General Remarks: These plants like warmer conditions than some other members of the Aralia family. They do well in central heating. They are not easy to propagate, but can be kept well if looked after carefully.

Species cultivated:

D. elegantissima (Syn. *Aralia elegantissima*) is the False Aralia and has thread-like drooping leaflets, the stalks being mottled with white.

D. Veitchii (Syn. *Aralia Veitchii*) has leaves which are dark red beneath.

DRACAENA

(Dragon Plant or Dragon Tree)

Ornamental foliage plants with leaves in various colours.

Propagation: (1) Cuttings of main stems or side shoots, 1 in. long and partially buried horizontally in compost in March.

(2) Root cuttings in March or April in temperature of 75 to 80 deg. F.

(3) Stem rooting in March or April.

(4) Offsets at any time.

(5) Seeds sown in March 1 in. deep in temperature of 85 deg. F.

Position: In the light, but varieties other than variegated ones may be given more shade.

Temperature: Warm.

Feeding: Feed once a week when established.

General Management: Re-pot in February or March using J.I.P.3. Can be transplanted more frequently if necessary, as it is a strong grower. Water moderately in winter and freely in summer. Syringe daily in summer.

General Remarks: This is an easy plant to grow and if it gets too big it can be cut right down. The bottom bit in the pot will carry on growing providing that it has a bud or two left, and the top portion can be inserted in a pot, where it will strike after a few weeks. Give plenty of air and space. It can go out in the garden in summer.

Species cultivated:

D. fragrans var. *Lindenii* has deep green leaves striped with yellow and pale yellow. · *D. fragans Massangeana* has broad leaves with a white stripe down the middle.

ELETTARIA

(Cardamon)

A perennial herb with creeping rhizome.

Cultivation: See Maranta.

Species cultivated:

E. cardamomum has green, downy-scented leaves and blue flowers with white stripes and yellow margins.

EUCALYPTUS

(Australian Gum-tree)

Some of the species are suitable for pot culture when they are young. The leaves are evergreen, covered with a greyish bloom and often pleasantly scented.

Propagation: Seeds sown in early spring in temperature of 65 deg. F. Also can be sown in August when tree is required to grow over the winter.

Position: In the full sun and can go in the garden in summer.

Temperature: Cool.

Feeding: Feed once a week with liquid manure when established.

General Management: Will need frequent re-potting in J.I.P.3. Water freely.

General Remarks: It will probably be found that the tree will have grown too large for the room in one season, so that it will have to be discarded. Propagation is not difficult.

Pruning: No pruning required.

Species cultivated:

E. citriodora, the Citron-scented Gum.

E. globulus, the Blue Gum.

EUCALYPTUS GLOBULUS.
Grows quickly and has " scented " leaves.

EURYA

A small evergreen shrub with tough laurel-like leaves.

Propagation: By cuttings of young shoots in spring in temperature of 60 to 65 deg. F.

Position: In the light but not strong sunlight.

Temperature: Cool.

General Management: Re-pot in March or April, planting firmly. Use J.I.P.1. Give plenty of drainage. Water freely in summer, but moderately in winter.

General Remarks: Likes plenty of space and air. Can go outside in summer. Syringe or wash over leaves from time to time.

Pruning: Is a slow grower and little pruning required.

Species cultivated:

E. japonica, var. *variegata*.

FATSHEDERA

This erect-growing shrubby plant has ivy-like leaves. It is a cross between Fatsia and Hedera.

Propagation: By cuttings in spring and summer over bottom heat. It is possible to propagate this at home in the summer.

Position: Prefers partial shade. Can be put out in shady spot in summer.

Temperature: Cool.

General Management: Re-pot in spring in J.I.P.2. Water freely in summer, but moderately to give rest in winter.

General Remarks: The variegated variety needs more light than the green-leaved form, which can go in a very shady corner. The plants need replacing every few years, as they are not at their best when old.

Pruning: Keep well pruned back to promote bushy growth.

FATSHERA LIZEI.

Species cultivated:

F. Lizei has green leaves, but there is a variegated form.

FATSIA

(Fig Leaf Palm or Japanese Aralia)

An evergreen shrub with dark green leathery leaves.

Propagation: (1) Seeds sown in temperature of 65 deg. F. in spring.

(2) Ripe cuttings of stems 2 ins. long in spring.

Position: In the light, but not direct sunlight. Can go in the shade.

Temperature: Moderate to cool.

General Management: Re-pot in spring, using J.I.P.3. Water freely in summer, but more moderately in winter. Feed once a week when established with liquid manure.

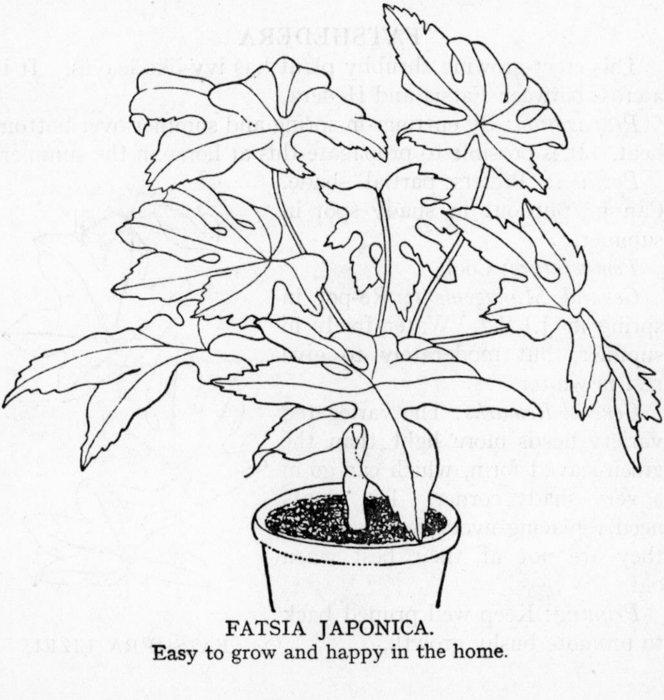

FATSIA JAPONICA.
Easy to grow and happy in the home.

AUCUBA JAPONICA
EASY TO GROW AND VERY GOOD IN FLATS.

PHILODENDRON SCANDENS
ONE OF THE NICEST CLIMBING PLANTS.

G neral Remarks: They make good room plants and should be kept, if possible, on the cool side.

Pruning: Prune hard in the spring to retain good shape.

Species cultivated:

F. japonica (Syn. *Aralia japonica, A Sieboldii*) has deep green shiny leaves. Var. *Moseri* is larger with more compact growth and var. *variegata* has white tips to the leaves.

FERNS

Flowerless plants grown for their foliage. Their deeply cut leaves are usually green, but often tinted with brown. Most ferns, being woodland plants, need the same general treatment, though as they come from different parts of the world, their temperature requirements are bound to differ.

Propagation: (1) Division of the plants in February or March.

(2) Bulbils for those species which form them.

(3) Spores as soon as they are ripe in a temperature of 55 to 75 deg. F.

(Ferns, with the exception of a few varieties, are not easy to propagate in the home).

Position: Not in the strong sunlight, and usually in the shade.

Feeding: Strong manures should never be used. A little weak liquid feeding may be given when the plants are well established.

General Management: Re-pot fairly firmly in the spring using J.I.P.2 and remove any old fronds. The roots may be pruned slightly if one does not wish to use a larger pot. Water freely in the summer but more moderately in the winter. During the winter the soil should not be too moist, neither should it dry out. The foliage should be syringed in hot weather and a moist atmosphere should be kept round the pots in summer.

General Remarks: Do not over-pot. They can be used for shady corners and where there is enough space for their foliage to be seen at its best. If the tap water is very alkaline, then rain water should be used.

Species cultivated:

There are many kinds grown, but only a few most commonly

cultivated will be mentioned here, with a few remarks to each

Adiantum (Maidenhair), var. *cuneatum* and many others. Has very graceful, dainty foliage of a bright green. This is probably only a temporary room plant. Do not syringe or water from overhead, but keep the roots moist. Prefers a light, airy atmosphere, but no sun.

Asplenium bulbiferum (Mother Spleenwort) has pretty dark-green fronds. The little bulblets on its leaves can be used for propagation. Prefers cool conditions and can go on for years in the home.

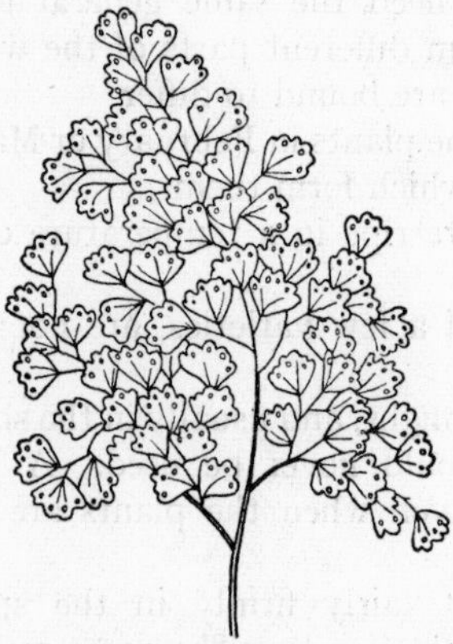

ADIANTUM CUNEATUM.
The Maidenhair Fern.

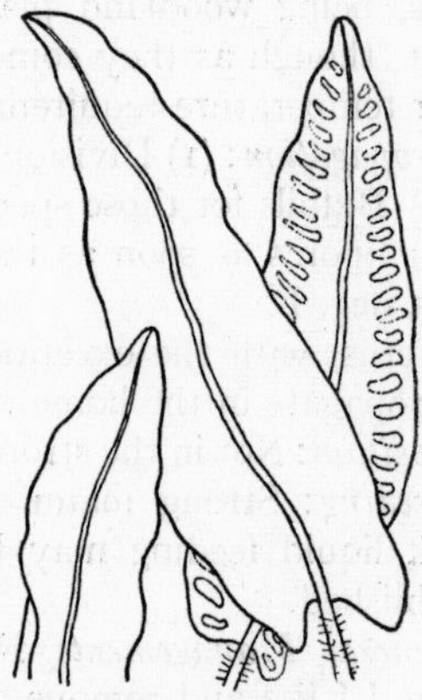

PHYLLITIS SCOLOPENDRIUM.

Nephrolepis Duffii and *exaltata* are two useful ferns. Keep well watered and feed from time to time. *N. Duffii* should be given plenty of room to develop. Both dislike draughts.

Phyllitis scolopendrium (Hart's-tongue) has long strap-shaped fronds. Can be propagated by division. Does well in a cool atmosphere and can tolerate shade.

Platycerium (Elk's-horn or Stag's-horn Fern) has a number of cultivated varieties, including *P. bifurcatum*, which is hardier than the others. Does well as a hanging or basket plant and is interesting as it grows into a kind of ball. Water well from underneath when the foliage starts to droop.

Pteris cretica and *P. tremula* make very good room plants. Division is the best means of propagation. They can do with more feeding than some ferns and are easy to grow and keep. They have dark green leathery fronds on slender stems.

FICUS

Evergreen shrub with decorative ornamental foliage.

(a) Cultivation for *Ficus elastica, F. australis* and similar species.

Propagation: (1) Cuttings of shoots in spring and summer in a temperature of 75 deg. F.

(2) " Eyes "—i.e., small pieces of stem about 1 in. long, containing a bud with a leaf attached, in a temperature of 75 deg. F.

(3) Stem rooting in spring.

(All the above methods need considerable temperatures and propagation is therefore difficult in the home.)

Position: Partial shade, but can be acclimatised to full sunlight. Can be put out in sheltered position in summer.

Temperature: February to October, warm to hot.

October to February, warm.

General Management: Pot or plant from February to April, using J.I.P.2. Water freely in summer, but moderately at other times.

General Remarks: They definitely prefer heat, but can get used to cooler conditions. Should be rested in the winter. Syringe daily in hot weather and wash the leaves from time to time. Do not over-water in winter, otherwise there is danger of the roots rotting.

Species cultivated:

F. elastica (India-rubber plant) has thick, glossy, elliptic, yellowish leaves. Var. *variegata* has variegated leaves.

F. elastica decora a particularly beautiful variety.

F. australis (Syn. *F. rubiginosa*) has leaves which are rusty and hairy underneath.

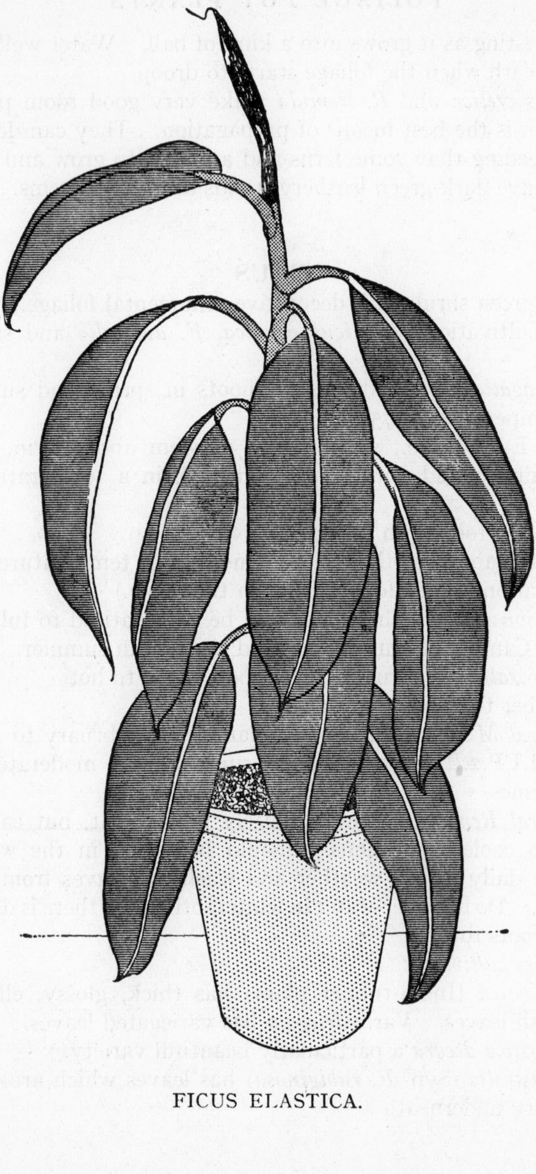

FICUS ELASTICA.

(b) Cultivation for *Ficus pumila* (Syn. *F. repens*), *F. radicans* and other similar species.

Propagation: By stem cuttings. (Can be done in the home provided that atmosphere is not too dry.)

Position: Partial shade, but will grow, if necessary, in quite deep shade.

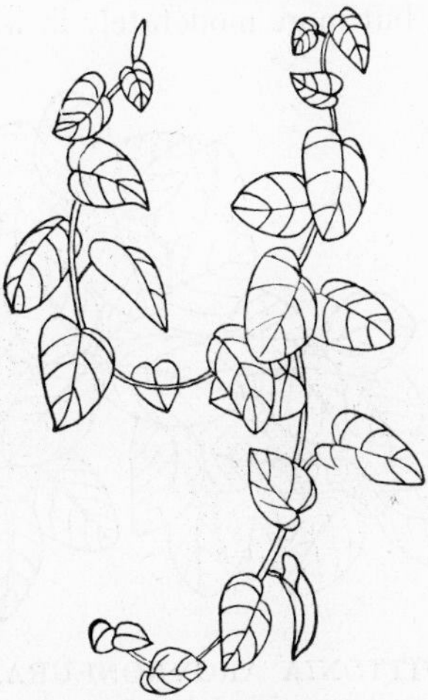

FICUS PUMILA.

Temperature: Moderate.

Feeding: An occasional feed with liquid manure.

General Management: Pot in smallish pots using J.I.P.2. Water freely in summer, more moderately in winter, but never let soil dry out. Syringe foliage from time to time. When the plant gets older, fig-type leaves will be borne at the top of the plant, cuttings taken from these will give large-leafed plants. They are easy to grow and quite hardy.

Species cultivated:

F. pumila (Syn. *F. repens*) is a small, green-leaved, creeping species. It is often called The Creeping Fig.

F. radicans is another small creeping species, but less hardy than *F. pumila*. Var. *variegata* has variegated foliage.

FITTONIA

Evergreen trailing plant with ornamental foliage.

Propagation: By cuttings of firm shoots from February to April in temperature of 75 to 85 deg. F. Strike easily.

Position: In the shade. Never in the sun.

Temperature: Warm.

General Management: Re-pot in spring using J.I.P.2. Water freely in summer, but more moderately in winter.

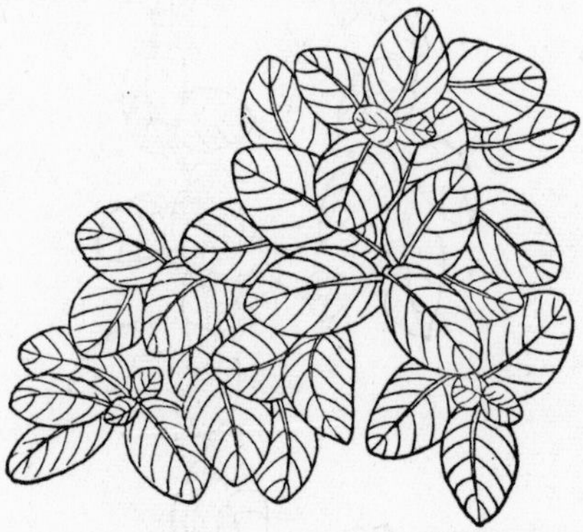

FITTONIA ARGYRONEURA.

General Remarks: This is not an easy plant for rooms and should be replaced from time to time. Syringe occasionally and keep out of draughts. Keep in small pots and ensure good drainage.

Species cultivated:

F. argyroneura has oval, bright green leaves, netted with white veins.

F. Verschaffeltii has dark green leaves, netted with deep red veins.

GREVILLEA

(Silk-bark Oak)

Evergreen shrub with feathery leaves. Orange flowers on older plants in summer.

Propagation: (1) Heel cuttings of young shoots 3 ins. long from March to May in a temperature of 75 to 80 deg. F.

(2) Seeds sown ½ in. deep in March in temperature of 65 to 75 deg. F. The seeds are large and flat and should be placed in the compost point downwards or sideways, but not flat.

Position: Prefers the sun, but also grows in partial shade. Can go out in garden in summer.

Temperature: Moderate, though can withstand warmer temperatures.

General Management: Re-pot firmly in March or April, using J.I.P.1. Water freely in summer, but keep rather dry in winter. Give plenty of air.

General Remarks: They are easily grown and make good plants for the house, as they can put up with central heating if needs be.

Pruning: No pruning on young plants.

Species cultivated:

G. robusta is the Silk-Oak and has orange flowers in summer. Grown mostly for its decorative, fern-like, silvery leaves.

HELXINE

(Baby's Tears)

A small, creeping moss-like plant with tiny matted, green leaves.

Propagation: By cuttings of the rooting shoots.

Position: Anywhere except in the bright sun. Garden in summer, if necessary.

Temperature: Cool.

General Management: Pot in J.I.P.2. Water well from underneath and never let pot dry out.

General Remarks: This little plant has often been used under greenhouse staging and as a ground or pot cover. If planted in a flat shallow pot it will soon spread and hang over the sides of the pot.

Species cultivated:

H. Soleirolii.

LIGULARIA

Plants with large green leaves blotched with yellow, white and sometimes light rose.

Propagation: By division of old plants. This can be done in the home.

Position: In the shade.

Temperature: Warm.

General Management: Re-pot when necessary in largish pots, using J.I.P.3. Water freely in summer and never let pot dry out completely.

General Remarks: Remove the flowers when they appear as they are not required. This plant loves water. Can be put out in garden in the summer.

Species cultivated:

L. Kaemferi var. *aureo-maculata* is the Leopard Plant. (Syn. *Farfugium grande, F. maculatum*).

MARANTA

(Arrowroot Plant)

Ornamental plant with leaves green on top and spotted with various colours.

Propagation: Division of plants in February or March.

Position: In the shade.

Temperature: Heat, but can tolerate cooler conditions.

Feeding: Feed plants occasionally during the summer.

General Management: Re-pot every year in March or April in J.I.P.2. Water copiously in spring and summer, less in autumn, and keep almost dry in winter. Syringe daily in summer.

General Remarks: Keep the atmosphere as moist as possible. Give rest during the winter months. Do not over-pot.

Species cultivated:

M. leuconeura has light green leaves with white midribs and veins. Red underneath. Var. *Kerchoveana* has larger leaves spotted with red underneath. Var. *Massangeana* has smaller leaves which are purple underneath.

MARANTA.
The Arrowroot Plant.
A plant beloved for its unusually marked leaves.

PANDANUS

(Screw Pine)

Evergreen shrubby plants with palm-shaped leaves.

Propagation: Suckers from February to April on bottom heat.

Position: In the sun or in good light.

Temperature: Warm.

General Management: Re-pot from January to April using J.I.P.1. Give good drainage, but keep to smallish pots. Do not feed. Water freely except in winter when give rest.

General Remarks: These plants do not like the cold and prefer a moist atmosphere. Syringe occasionally. Water carefully when young. The old plants look like a " screw ".

Species cultivated:

P. Veitchii is the most commonly cultivated and has white banded leaves, with silvery-white margins.

PEPEROMIA

(Pepper Elder)

Creeping perennial plant with ornamental foliage.

Propagation: By cuttings of shoots, or a single joint with leaf attached, in spring with bottom heat, and a temperature of 65 to 75 deg. F.

Position: Partial shade.

Temperature: Warm, but can acclimatise themselves to average room temperatures.

General Management: Re-pot in March or April using J.I.P.1. Give good drainage and use smallish pots. Water moderately in winter and freely in summer. Syringe occasionally in summer.

General Remarks: Some can be grown as hanging plants, When rooting-joints are produced they can be propagated at home. Keep out of draughts. Do not use cold water for watering.

Species cultivated:

P. Sandersii var. *argyrea* is one of the hardiest and has green and white leaves, with lighter patches between the veins.

P. tithymaloides (Syn. *P. magnoliaefolia*) has yellow, cream and green leaves.

PILEA

Dwarf foliage plants with small green leaves and insignificant flowers.

Propagation: By cuttings from January to May in temperature of 65 to 75 deg. F.

Position: Partial shade.

Temperature: Warm in summer, moderate in winter.

General Management: Re-pot from February to April using J.I.P.2. Small pots. Water freely in summer, more sparingly at other times.

General Remarks: They are not really suitable for rooms heated by gas or paraffin.

Species cultivated:

P. microphylla (Syn. *P. muscosa*) is the Artillery Plant and has tiny leaves. When dry the pollen is discharged forcibly.

P. nummulariaefolia—Creeping Charley—is useful as a hanging plant.

P. Cadierei is a small plant with green and silver mottled leaves.

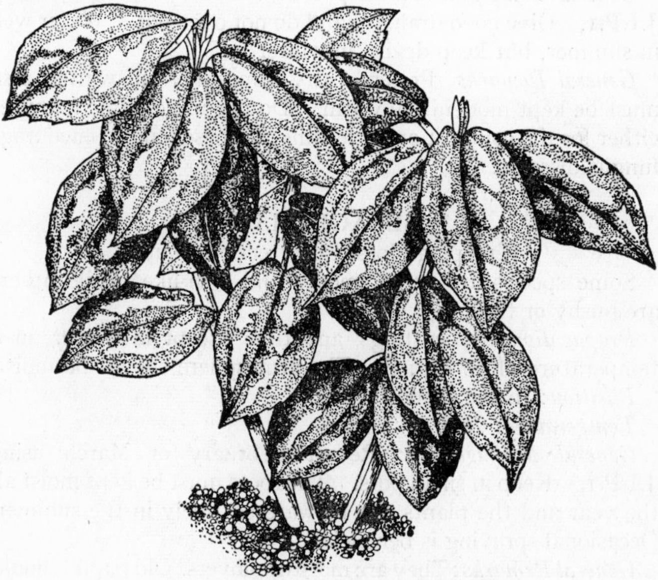

PILEA CADIEREI.
An interesting "easy to grow" plant.

RHOEO discolor

(Syn. *Tradescantia discolor* and *versicolor*) is similar to the Tradescantia, but larger. The leaves are dark-green above and purple below. The flowers are insignificant.

Cultivation: See Tradescantia.

SANSEVIERIA

(Bow-string Hemp)

Ornamental foliage plants. The flowers, which are whitish or yellowish, are insignificant.

Propagation: (1) Division of plants from February to April. (2) Leaf-cuttings about three inches long in sand.

Position: In the sun, but can tolerate partial shade.

Temperature: Moderate.

Feeding: Feed once a week during growing season.

General Management: Re-pot in February or April using J.I.P.1. Give good drainage and do not over-pot. Water well in summer, but keep dryish in winter.

General Remarks: Prefers a dry atmosphere in winter, also must be kept moderately warm. Do not use organic manures either for the compost or for feeding, as these tend to encourage fungus diseases.

SELAGINELLA

(Creeping Moss, Resurrection Plant)

Some species are green, mossy and fern-like, while others are bushy or trailing.

Propagation: By cuttings, any time except in winter, in a temperature of 70 deg. F. The atmosphere should be moist.

Position: In the shade.

Temperature: Cool.

General Management: Re-pot February or March using J.I.P.1. Keep in small pots. The roots must be kept moist all the year and the plants can be watered freely in the summer. Occasional spraying is beneficial.

General Remarks: They are moisture-lovers. Old plants should be discarded from time to time and new ones grown in their place.

Species cultivated:

S. lepidophylla is the Resurrection Plant. It curls up when dry and expands again if moistened.

S. Martensii is one of the most commonly grown. Var. *variegata* has white markings.

S. Kraussiana has creeping rooting stems and is often used for hanging baskets.

SYNGONIUM

A creeping tropical plant with green arrow-shaped leaves, having whitish midribs.

Propagation: Cuttings with bottom heat.

Position: Partial shade.

Temperature: Warm.

Feeding: Feed once a week with liquid manure during growing season.

General Management: Pot in J.I.P.2. Water well during growing season, but more sparingly otherwise.

General Remarks: May be grown up moss-covered canes with support. It is difficult to propagate without bottom heat, but makes a good room plant as it requires little light.

Species cultivated:

S. podophyllum var. *albolineatum.*

TRADESCANTIA

(Spiderwort)

Small creeping plants with ornamental striped leaves.

Propagation: By cuttings. Can be done at almost any time in the home.

Position: Not direct sunlight. Variegated varieties hold their colours best in the light.

Temperature: Moderate.

Feeding: Feed occasionally when established.

General Management: Re-pot in J.I.P.2 as necessary. Water well in summer, but less at other times. Never allow to get quite dry.

General Remarks: They are very easy to grow and make excellent house plants. They should be cheap to buy in the first place and simple to propagate afterwards. Syringe occasionally. The flowers are insignificant. Can be put outside in summer in shade.

Species cultivated:

T. fluminensis is probably the most commonly grown. Var. *variegata* has small leaves striped with yellow and white. This species is often confused with *Zebrina pendula* which has leaves that are purple underneath. *T. fluminensis* is the

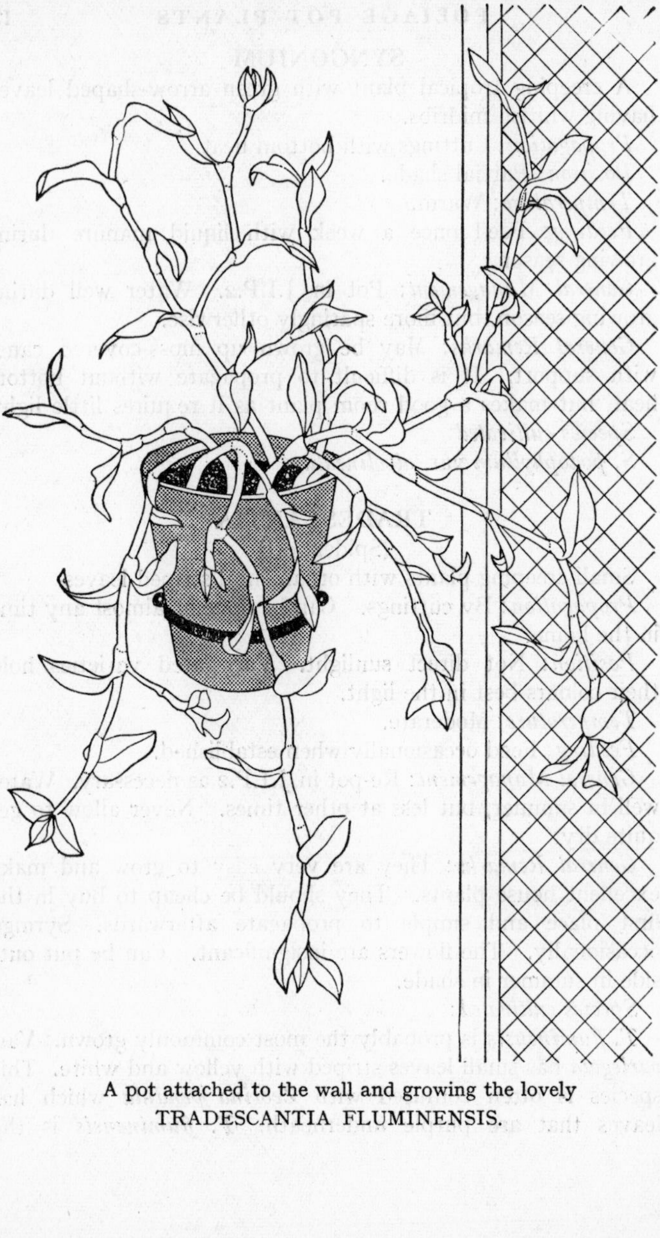

A pot attached to the wall and growing the lovely
TRADESCANTIA FLUMINENSIS.

Wandering Jew (Syn. *T. albiflora, T. striata, T. tricolor* and *T. virdis*).

ZEBRINA pendula

Has fleshier leaves than *Tradescantia fluminensis.* The leaves striped with white on top are purple underneath.

Cultivation: As for Tradescantia, but can support warmer conditions.

ZEBRINA PENDULA.

CHAPTER 13

FOLIAGE POT PLANTS FOR USE AS HANGING PLANTS

AMPELOPSIS
(Baby Virginian Creeper)

A DECIDUOUS, tendril-climbing plant with green and red leaves. The flowers are insignificant.

Propagation: (1) By soft wood cuttings in the summer. (2) By layering, which can be done in the home.

Position: In partial shade. Can go outside in summer.

Temperature: Cool.

General Management: Re-pot in spring, using J.I.P.2. Water moderately and do not over-water. Keep in smallish pots.

General Remarks: They make useful hanging plants and can tolerate cool conditions. Be careful of Red Spider. Can also be propagated by cuttings in water.

Pruning: Prune well back after resting period in winter, before bringing into warmer conditions.

Species cultivated:

A. brevipedunculata has heart-shaped leaves. The variety *elegans* has leaves variegated with white, green or pink.

ASPARAGUS *Sprengeri*

Makes a very useful hanging plant. For cultivation, see Asparagus in Chapter 12.

CHLOROPHYTUM *comosum*

Is a good hanging plant when older. For cultivation, see Chapter 12.

NEPHTHYTIS

Plant with creeping rhizome and arrow-shaped leaves.

Propagation: By cuttings on bottom heat in spring.

Position: Partial shade.

Temperature: Warm.

General Management: Pot or plant in J.I.P.2. Water freely in summer, moderately in winter. Syringe daily in summer.

General Remarks: Makes quite a good room plant as it can be grown well in the shade, if required. Prefers a moist atmosphere.

Species cultivated:

N. Afzelii is the species. Var. *variegata* has variegated foliage.

OPLISMENUS

A grass having spiked leaves in various colours.

Propagation: By stem wherever they touch the soil.

Position: Partial shade, but prefers more light during winter months.

Temperature: Warm.

Feeding: Feed once a week with liquid manure when established.

General Management: Pot in J.I.P.2. Water freely during summer and more moderately in winter, though always keep fairly moist.

General Remarks: Syringe frequently. Old plants should be discarded and young ones propagated. Propagation is very easy.

Species cultivated:

O. hirtellus has a variegated leaved form (Syn. *Panicum variegatum*).

O. Burmannii variegatus is a good variety.

PILEA *nummulariaefolia*

(Creeping Charley)

A good hanging plant.

Cultivation: See Chapter 12.

SAXIFRAGA

(Strawberry Geranium)

The species *sarmentosa* (Syn. *Sekika sarmentosa*), (the Strawberry Geranium), is commonly used as a hanging plant. It has long, slender and trailing shoots, with tiny plantlets here and there all over the plant.

Propagation: (1) Division in spring.

(2) Plantlets potted up singly in spring and summer.

Position: In the light, but not in direct sun.

Temperature: Cool.

General Management: Re-pot in March or April using J.I.P.2. Water freely during growing season, but keep drier in winter.

General Remarks: A good hanging plant, easy to propagate in the home.

Species cultivated:

S. sarmentosa.

SCIRPUS

(Bulrush)

Grass-like plant with flowers in little spikelets.

Propagation: By division.

Position: Partial shade.

Temperature: Warm.

General Remarks: Grow in J.I.P.2. Water freely at all times. In fact can always stand in a saucer filled with water. Syringe foliage from time to time.

General Remarks: Quite a useful hanging plant, which can be propagated in the home.

Species cultivated:

S. cernuus has threadlike drooping stems, which are almost leafless (Syn. *Isolepis gracilis*).

SELAGINELLA *Kraussiana*

Is often used as a hanging plant. For cultivation see Chapter 12.

SENECIO

(German Ivy)

The species *mikanioides* is the one used as a hanging plant.

Propagation: By cuttings of the running shoots.

Position: In the sun.

Temperature: Moderate to cool.

Feeding: Feed once a week when established with liquid manure.

General Management: Re-pot in J.I.P.2 in spring. Water freely during growing period, more moderately otherwise.

General Remarks: The flowers should be pinched out as they are not required. It is easy to grow and not much trouble to look after.

Species cultivated:

S. mikanioides.

STENOTAPHRUM

(St. Augustine Grass)

Creeping grass with little white spiked leaves.

Propagation: By runners.

Position: Partial shade.

Temperature: Moderate.

General Management: Pot or plant in J.I.P.2. Water fairly freely.

General Remarks: This plant is one of the easiest to grow and is very useful either as a hanging plant or for an edging in front of other plants.

Species cultivated:

Stenotaphrum secundatum (Syn. *S. americanum*) var. *variegatum* has white striped leaves.

TRADESCANTIA *fluminensis* and **ZEBRINA** *pendula* both make, of course, good hanging plants. See Chapter 11.

CHAPTER 14

CLIMBING POT PLANTS

BEFORE 1939 few people in Britain grew climbing plants in their houses. Today, however, maybe as the result of the Danish and Swedish influence, they have become very popular and rightly so.

This chapter contains a list of climbing pot plants considered suitable for growing in the house. Plants, which are either rampant growers or very difficult to cultivate, have not been included.

Please note especially the statements made in each case under the heading *General Remarks*.

CISSUS

A climbing plant with ornamental leaves, usually climbing by means of tendrils.

Propagation: (1) *C. striata* by cuttings or half-ripe wood on slight bottom heat.

(2) *C. gongylodes* by means of the terminal fleshy tubers, which are produced on the branches at the end of the growing season. These can be potted up. Also by cuttings in spring.

Position: In partial shade. Suitable for growing up trellis-work in pots.

Temperature: Moderate.

Feeding: Feed occasionally with weak liquid manure during full growth.

General Management: Re-pot in spring using J.I.P.2. Give good drainage. Water freely in summer, but more sparingly in winter to give rest.

General Remarks: *C. striata* is a slow grower and does well in a small pot. *C. gongylodes* is one of the most rapid growing vines, but can be kept well in hand by pruning, *C. antartica* is very popular.

Species cultivated:

C. striata (Syn. *Vitis striata*) has feathery downy leaves and slender tendrils.

C. gongylodes has larger leaves or long stalks. The leaves are sometimes three-lobed.

COBEA

(Cup and Saucer Plant or Mexican Ivy)

An easily grown climber with large bell-shaped flowers.

Time of flowering: Summer.

Propagation: Seeds sown in March in slight heat. Fresh seed must be used.

Position: Will tolerate partial shade, but needs light for flowering.

Temperature: Warm during summer, moderate in winter.

Feeding: Feed once a week with liquid manure during summer.

General Management: Pot in March using J.I.P.2 and largish pots. Water freely in spring and summer, but moderately at other times.

General Remarks: It is possible to use them purely as foliage plants away from the window, where they are not likely to flower. It is probably best to discard the old plants, though they can be kept. Propagation is fairly easy, though perhaps it is advisable to stratify the seeds by soaking them well before sowing. Only keep the best seedlings.

Species cultivated:

C. scandens has flowers which are green inside and violet outside. There is also a variegated form, which is usually raised from cuttings.

HEDERA

(Ivy)

The well-known climbing plant with dark-green leathery leaves.

A pewter pot on a mantelpiece growing a dwarf " Ivy " or Hedera.

Propagation: (1) By cuttings over slight bottom heat in spring.

(2) By cuttings in summer without heat.

Position: In the shade, but not too much shade for variegated varieties. Can go out in garden in summer in shade.

Temperature: Any ordinary room temperature.

General Management: Pot in J.I.P.1, using small pots for the variegated varieties and larger ones for the green ones. Water freely in summer, more moderately at other times.

General Remarks: Should be syringed from time to time. These plants are very little trouble and adapt themselves to most room conditions.

Species cultivated:

Hedera Helix is really the common Ivy which has a number of forms:

H. Helix sagittaefolia has arrow-shaped leaves.

H. Helix digitata, has deeply lobed leaves.

H. Helix marginata, has leaves with cream or yellow margins.

H. Helix glacier, a white leaved variety

Hedera Helix Canariensis (*fol.* var.) a golden yellow leaved kind.

HOYA

(Honey-plant or Wax Flower)

An evergreen climber, with thick leaves and wheel-shaped flowers in clusters.

Time of flowering: Summer.

Propagation: (1) Cuttings of shoots of the previous year's growth from March to May in a temperature of 75 to 85 deg. F.

(2) Layering shoots in spring and summer (propagation is not easy to do in the home).

Position: Not in the direct sunlight, but does not want too deep shade.

Temperature: Warm. Can go outside in summer in shady, warm, spot.

General Management: Pot or plant in February or March. Water freely in spring or summer, moderately at other times. Do not over-pot, give good drainage and use J.I.P.1.

General Remarks: Can be grown up small trellis-work in pots. Do not feed just before it is coming into flower. Give good ventilation.

Pruning: Very mild pruning to shape in February.

Species cultivated:

H. bella has pale pink and white flowers.

H. carnosa (Wax Flower) has deep pink and red flowers.

IPOMOEA
(Morning Glory)

Climbers with convolvulus-like flowers, each lasting only a short time.

Time of flowering: Summer or winter.

Propagation: By seeds sown in March or April in a temperature of 60 deg. F. Put two or three seeds in a pot. Can be done in the home.

Position: Full sunlight.

Temperature: Moderate to warm.

General Management: Pot from February to April, using J.I.P.1. Water freely in spring and summer, more moderately at other times.

General Remarks: Can be grown up small trellis work in a pot. It is very easy to grow and needs little looking-after. Do not over-pot. Can be put out in the garden on warm days.

Species cultivated:

I. Horsfalliae has deep rose flowers in winter.

There are numerous other species and varieties cultivated. e.g., *I. rubur coertulea* var. Heavenly Blue, flowers in summer.

MANETTIA

An evergreen climber with small scarlet and orange flowers.

Time of flowering: March to December.

Propagation: By cuttings of young shoots 2 to 3 ins. long in summer in a temperature of 65 to 75 deg. F.

Position: Good light, but not full sunlight.

Temperature: Cool.

General Management: Pot in February or March in J.I.P.1. Water freely in spring and summer, but more moderately at other times. Syringe daily during the summer months.

General Remarks: Is suitable for growing on trellis-work stuck in its pot. Give plenty of ventilation.

Pruning: Cut back lightly after flowering.

Species cultivated:

M. bicolor has bright scarlet and yellow flowers.

MAURANDIA

Perennial climbing plant with numerous flowers in a range of colours. The flowers are funnel-shaped.

Time of flowering: Summer and autumn.

Propagation: (1) By seeds in spring on slight bottom heat. (2) By cuttings in August under close conditions. (Can be propagated in the home).

Position: In the full sun and can go outside in the summer.

Temperature: Cool.

General Management: Is best grown as an annual, but when keeping plant, re-pot in spring using J.I.P.1. Water freely in summer, but moderately in winter.

General Remarks: Can be grown up trellis work stuck in a pot. Syringe occasionally. Quick grower.

Species cultivated:

M. Barclaiana has flowers in colours ranging from white and rose to deep purple. There are a number of named varieties.

MONSTERA

Evergreen climber with large ornamental, dark green leaves. The yellow flowers are followed by edible fruits, which have a pineapple flavour.

Time of flowering: Summer.

Propagation: By cuttings of stems at any time in a temperature of 70 to 80 deg. F. The atmosphere must be moist (not suitable for propagation in the home).

Position: Not in the full sunlight and will tolerate shady conditions.

Temperature: Warm to hot.

General Management: Re-pot February to April in J.I.P.3. Water freely in spring and summer, but moderately at other times. Foliage should be frequently sprayed over in summer.

General Remarks: This plant will grow very large, if allowed, but can be kept well cut back. Keep in as small a pot as possible to give restricted root room, where it is desired to keep the plant small. It appreciates feeding during the summer. Keep out of draughts.

Species cultivated:

M. deliciosa is the most commonly cultivated species and has a number of cultivated varieties suitable for house plants.

PHILODENDRON

Ornamental, evergreen climbing shrub with leathery green leaves in various shapes. One of the best-known foliage plants for the house.

Propagation: By cuttings of stems in temperature of 75 deg. F. at any time. The cuttings root quite easily.

Position: Very adaptable, but prefers partial shade. Can tolerate very shady conditions.

Temperature: Warm

General Management: Re-pot from January to April using J.I.P.3. Water freely in summer and soil should always be kept moist during the winter. Syringe frequently.

General Remarks: They are grown in great quantities in the United States as house plants. They prefer the warmth and dislike draughts. They can be grown up a trellis work and some varieties prefer to support themselves on a moss-covered stick. Their propagation is best left to the nurseryman, unless facilities are available to provide considerable heat.

Species cultivated:

P. scandens (Syn. *P. cuspidatum*, *P. micans* and *P. oxycardium*) has heart-shaped leaves and is one of the most commonly grown.

P. erubescens has arrow-shaped reddish leaves. Quick-growing, and has aerial roots at almost every joint.

RHOICISSUS

An evergreen, climbing vine. The leaves are reddish and hairy at first, but later become almost glabrous.

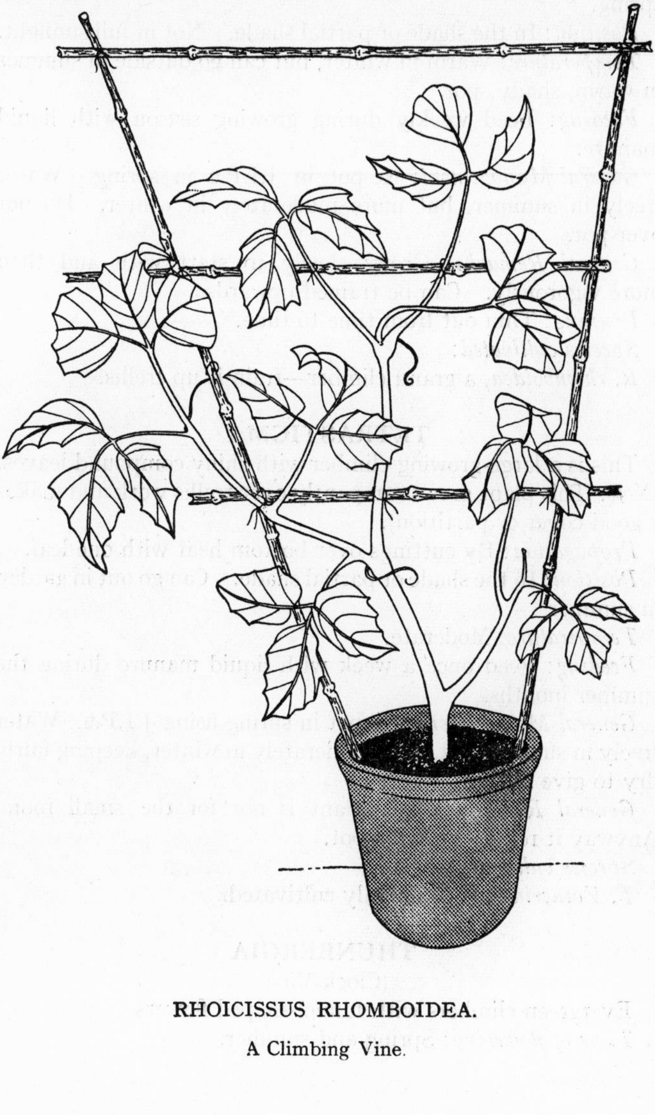

RHOICISSUS RHOMBOIDEA.

A Climbing Vine.

Propagation: By stem cuttings on slight bottom heat in spring.

Position: In the shade or partial shade. Not in full sunlight.

Temperature: Warm in winter, but can go outside in summer in warm, shady spot.

Feeding: Feed weekly during growing season with liquid manure.

General Management: Re-pot in J.I.P.2 in spring. Water freely in summer, but more moderately in winter. Do not over-pot.

General Remarks: Grows slowly to start with and then more vigorously. Can be trained upwards.

Pruning: Thin out from time to time.

Species cultivated:

R. rhomboidea, a grand climber—train it up trellis.

TETRASTIGMA

This is a large-growing climber with shiny compound leaves. (*Note*. This plant grows rampantly over trellis work and makes a good cover or partition).

Propagation: By cuttings over bottom heat with one leaf.

Position: In the shade or partial shade. Can go out in garden in summer.

Temperature: Moderate.

Feeding: Feed once a week with liquid manure during the summer months.

General Management: Re-pot in spring using J.I.P.2. Water freely in summer but more moderately in winter, keeping fairly dry to give resting period.

General Remarks: This plant is not for the small room. Anyway it requires a large pot.

Species cultivated:

T. Voineriana is commonly cultivated.

THUNBERGIA

(Clock Vine)

Evergreen climbers with funnel-shaped flowers.

Time of flowering: Spring and summer.

Propagation: (1) *T. alata* can easily be raised by seeds sown in April and May. Two or three to the 5 in. pot.

(2) *T. grandiflora* is raised from cuttings in a temperature of 75 to 85 deg. F.

Position: In the sun.

Temperature: *T. grandiflora* requires warmer conditions than *T. alata*, which can go out in the summer.

General Management: Pot in J.I.P.2 in February or March, giving good drainage. Water well in summer, but moderately in winter. Do not allow *T. grandiflora* to become water-logged.

General Remarks: *T. alata* is often grown as an annual owing to the ease with which it can be propagated. Give plenty of room and air to both species.

Pruning: *T. grandiflora* should be pruned back slightly after flowering.

Species cultivated:

T. alata has yellow flowers with purple spot below.

T. grandiflora has large blue flowers. This species does need quite a considerable amount of room.

CHAPTER 15

THE BULBS AND CORMS

THE growing of bulbs and corms in the house is undoubtedly one of the simplest of all forms of pot plant culture. My elder son, who is now the Senior Lecturer on the Staff of the Thaxted Horticultural Training College, potted up his own daffodils when he was only eight years of age and grew them so well that he won a prize for them at school. In fact, this school adopted the whole scheme of bulb growing in order to encourage their young people to take an interest in pot plant culture in the home. The housewife generally prefers bowls to pots, because she can then place them on table-cloths or on polished furniture without causing any marks. A bulb certainly looks well in bowls of a fair depth, but these should be of a plain colour, preferably dark green or terra-cotta.

Many different kinds of bulbs can be grown indoors, but the easiest perhaps are Tulips, Hyacinths, Narcissi (including of course the Daffodils), Scillas, Crocuses and Snowdrops. Irises might be included, but unfortunately they don't like being moved about from place to place and they often refuse to flower in consequence.

There are the later flowering bulbs and corms such as Gladioli, Freesias and Lilies, but these are on the whole more difficult to grow. Whatever type of bulb or corm is going to be grown, it pays to buy specimens which are well developed and of a good flowering size.

Most householders like to grow their bulbs in sedge peat or fibre. Both of these substances are clean to handle and hold the moisture well. Further they do not damage the inside of a nice porcelain bowl. Some people like to mix a little oyster-shell with the fibre, plus a small portion of charcoal, and the latter is said to keep the fibre or peat sweet. Anyway,

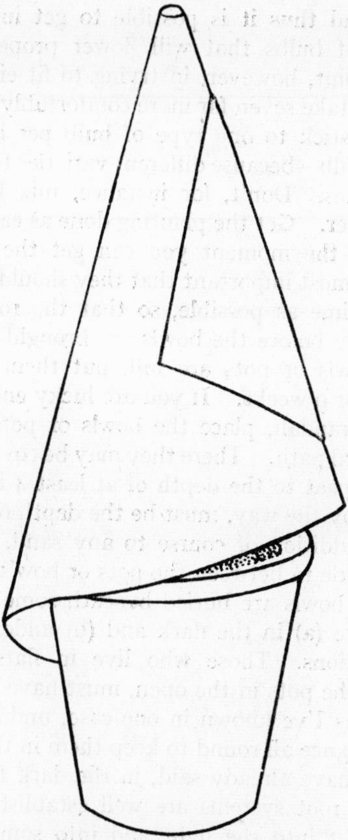

A paper dunces cap put over a growing hyacinth to draw it up.

it is necessary to thoroughly moisten the organic matter which is used in the bowl, and this should be done first of all in a galvanised bucket or bath, by having plenty of boiling water poured over it. It is only when it is soaked that the fibre can be pressed down well, so as to drain the excess moisture away. It is then in the right condition for using.

The bulbs can be planted so that they just do not touch

one another, and thus it is possible to get into the bowl a large number of bulbs that will flower properly. There is obviously no point, however, in trying to fit eight bulbs into a bowl that will take seven far more comfortably and naturally. It is better to stick to one type of bulb per bowl and even one variety of bulb—because different varieties tend to come up at differing dates. Don't, for instance, mix Hyacinths and Daffodils together. Get the planting done as early as you can, that is to say, the moment you can get the bulbs for the purpose. It is most important that they should be in the dark for as long a time as possible, so that the root system can develop properly before the bowls are brought into the light.

Once the bowls or pots are full, put them somewhere in the dark for 8 or 9 weeks. If you are lucky enough to have a garden or a verandah, place the bowls or pots here on concrete or on a hard path. There they may be covered with sand, ashes or sedge peat to the depth of at least 4 inches. This 4 inch covering, by the way, must be the depth over the tops of the bowls, in addition of course to any sand, ashes or peat, which may trickle in between the pots or bowls.

See that the bowls are buried beneath some such material; so that they are (a) in the dark and (b) undergo the normal climatic conditions. Those who live in flats, and cannot, therefore, put the pots in the open, must have them in a dark cupboard, or, as I've known in one case, underneath the bed with a deep valance all round to keep them in the dark. They are kept, as I have already said, in the dark for 8 weeks—at least until the root systems are well established. They can then be brought into the light and into some heat. When bowls are kept in a cupboard or under a bed, they have to be watered from time to time, so as to prevent the peat or fibre from drying out. Care must be taken never to over-water.

There is no reason at all why the bulbs shouldn't be grown in soil, except that it isn't so clean to handle as sedge peat. An ordinary flower pot should be used, and this should be properly crocked first. The bulbs are then planted in a similar manner as described for fibre, and should be kept in the dark for the 8 or 9 weeks. Some people grow their bulbs in boxes

THE VIBURNUM TINUS
IS BELOVED FOR ITS SCENTED MASS OF BLOSSOMS.

FUCHSIA

THERE ARE MANY VARIETIES TO CHOOSE FROM—AND EASY TO GROW ALSO.

or pots, and then, when growth has well-developed, the plants are transferred into the bowls in which they are going to be displayed in the house. The advantage of this method is that one can always pot up into a bowl bulbs which are at the same stages of growth.

Certain bulbs, and especially Hyacinths, can be grown in water, and special tall hyacinth glasses can be bought for this purpose. The bulbs " sit " in the niche made for them, but not actually in the water, and the roots go down into the water. One or two pieces of charcoal are usually put into the container below, so that the water is kept sweet. As the roots use the water, more and more is added from time to time. Once again the bulbs are kept in the dark for at least 8 weeks. In fact, it is never wise to bring the bulbs out into the light until the roots have grown down well into the glass vase.

DAFFODILS AND NARCISSI

It is important with daffodils and narcissi to plant early but shallowly. If the bulbs are not made firm the mass of roots may lift them from their place. Cover them for 12 to 16 weeks preferably and they will then flower in a uniform and natural manner. They should not be forced, a temperature of 45 deg. F. is ample, plus plenty of fresh air. When the flower buds are visible it is possible to increase to 55 deg. F.

Keep the fibre or sedge peat damp all the time and when bowls are out of doors covered to a depth of 6 inches with sedge peat, sand or leaf mould, this covering should be kept damp but not wet. If there should be a very rainy winter it may be necessary to cover the bulbs up with a piece of tarpaulin for water must never be allowed to stand in the bottom of the bowls.

Varieties Daffodils

(a) *Yellow trumpets.* Golden Harvest, Golden Spur, King Alfred, Covent Garden.

(b) *Bi-color trumpets.* Celebrity, Foresight, President Lebrun, Queen of the Bicolors.

(c) *White Trumpets.* Beersheba, Mount Hood, Gloria.

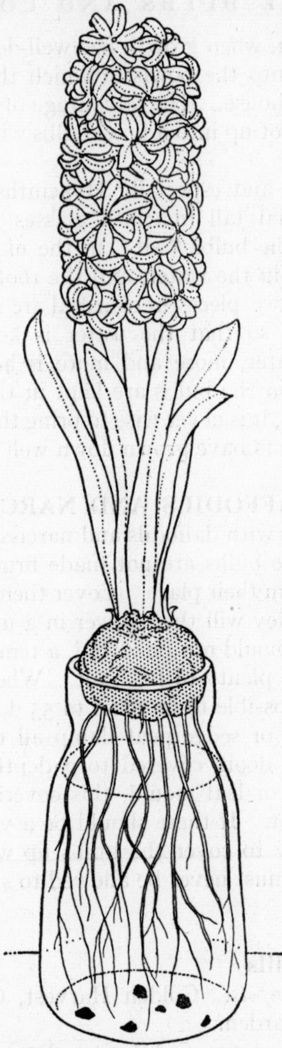

A HYACINTH growing in a glass vase filled with water. Note the charcoal at the bottom.

Varieties Narcissi

(a) *Large Cupped.* Carlton, Fortune, Crocus, Monte Carlo, Scarlet Elegance. Orange Bride, Red Bird, White Nile.

(b) *Small Cupped.* Firetail, Pomona, Verger, White Queen.

(c) *Double.* Eggs and Bacon, Insulinde, Twink.

(d) *Jonquils.* Waterperry, Trevithian.

(e) *Poetaz.* Abundance, Cragford, Halvose, Scarlet Gem.

N.B. Nearly all the Poetaz types need to be very gently forced and in fact the variety Cheerfulness cannot be gently forced until after the middle of February.

HYACINTHS

Those who want very early hyacinths have to buy what are called " Prepared " bulbs. These may be grown quite happily without the aid of a greenhouse. They will have been put into cold store for a time and because of this can be got into bloom by Christmas if necessary. They must be planted in their bowls by the middle of September and they should then go into the dark at a temperature of about 60 deg. F. where they should remain until the little flowers are well above the neck of the bowl. On the whole some people think they are a little more difficult to do than the ordinary hyacinths.

Normal hyacinths are treated in a similar manner to daffodils (please see page 150) and if the bowls are buried outside it is possible to prevent them from becoming dirty with the ashes or peat used by wrapping them in newspaper first. This never impedes the top growth of the bulbs. When the hyacinth has thrown up its spikes it is possible to bring the bowl into the house. If 2 or 3 spikes appear the side one should be cut off at the lowest point possible, or if a second spike comes out from the centre it can be pulled out with some force.

There are over 40 different varieties of hyacinths and they can be roughly divided into 3 groups. The first, the Early Roman Hyacinths, the second, the True Hyacinths, and the third, the Cynthella which can be forced from the middle of January onwards. These latter hyacinths have lovely loose spikes and are quite different from the others. Normal hyacinths are planted in sedge peat or fibre as for daffodils and if one bulb in a bowl looks as if it is growing a bit slower than another, it is possible to make a dunce's cap with paper and put it over the top of this specimen to hasten growth.

Varieties

(a) *Roman.* There are no varieties as far as I know.

(b) *True Hyacinths.* Hoare Frost, a white, Yellowhammer, Garibaldi, crimson, red, Lady Derby, a pale pink, Princess Irene, a rose pink, Duke of Westminster, a purple blue, Myosotis a pale sky blue, Winston Churchill, an outstanding sky blue. Purple King.

(c) *Cynthella.* Cape Town, a bright pink; Grace Darling, a sky blue; Morning Star, a yellow; The Bride, a pure white.

TULIPS

The best time to pot tulips is undoubtedly late September or early October. Each year they should have new potting soil and the bowls or pots chosen must be placed in a shady spot so that they can be covered with at least 6 inches of sand, ashes or sedge peat. It is important to allow the tops to grow to a height of 4 inches before bringing them into the home or greenhouse. When they are brought indoors, they are best kept in the dark for 3 weeks at a temperature of 60 deg. F. to allow the stems to lengthen. Then they are brought out into the light. It is important never to hurry tulips on the other hand they should be well watered, if they are earlies, but kept on the dry side if they are Darwins.

Tulips are apt to go blind if hurried and they may not flower because of draughts in the room or because they receive too much heat in the early stages. There are three main types of tulips, the single earlies, the doubles and the Darwins. The Darwins grow very tall and are not suitable for small houses.

Varieties

(a) *Single Earlies.* Brilliant Star, a scarlet; Flamingo, a soft pink.; Mon Tresor, a bright yellow; Peter Pan, a rose pink and cream; Prince of Austria, a flaming red with orange glow.

(b) *Double tulips.* Golden King, Jan Steen, an orange

THE TULIP YELLOW PRINCE.

Growing in a black bowl.

yellow with stripes of red; Aga Khan, an orange and golden yellow; Murillo, a pale pink; Peach Blossom; Scarlet Cardinal; Toreador, a dull crimson and buff orange.

(c) *Darwins.* General Eisenhower, a glorious red; Afterglow, a deep orange; Bartigon, a rosy red; Farncombe Sanders, a rich red; Princess Elizabeth, a deep pink with white base; William Pitt, a deep scarlet; Zina, a golden yellow.

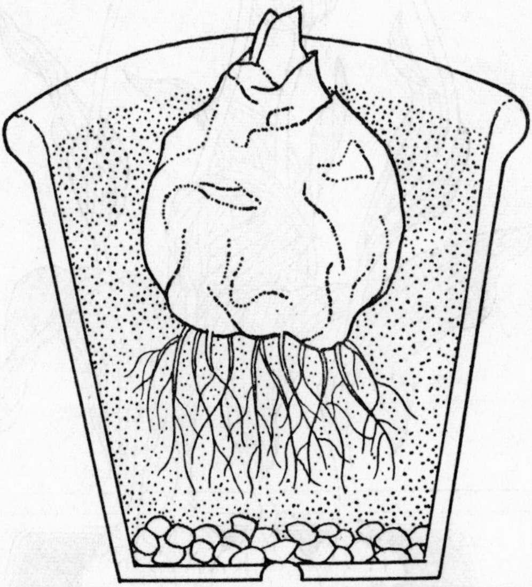

A Tulip bulb growing in a well crocked pot.

SCILLAS

The bulbs are quite small and may be massed in bowls. The plants only grow 4 or 5 inches high. Don't buy *Scilla nutans*, as this is the common bluebell of our woods.

Try instead:

Scilla bifolia, a bright blue which comes out in March.

Scilla siberica. Spring Beauty, a rich Prussian blue.

SNOWDROPS

These should be planted fairly thickly in shallow pots or bowls, and must be kept in the dark for at least 8 weeks.

Try:

Galanthus nivalis, the ordinary snowdrop.

Galanthus nivalis Flore pleno, the double snowdrop.

CHIONODOXAS

These can be grown quite easily in bowls and are early flowering. They need about 8 weeks in the dark before being brought into a warm room. Plant the bulbs an inch apart.

I have grown the following with success indoors:

Chionodoxa sardensis, dark blue small flowers.

Chionodoxa gigantea, lavender blue, large.

CROCUS

You often get four flowers to a crocus bulb. Plant them up the moment the bulbs arrive and keep them in the dark until the middle of December. Bring them indoors at that time and place them in a room as near the light as possible. Always keep them away from too much heat, but water them regularly.

Good varieties to try are:

Snowstorm, a pure white with an orange stigma.

Maximilian, a pale lilac.

Purpurea grandiflora, large deep purple flowers.

OTHER BULBS

It is possible of course to grow Irises, Tritonias, Gladoli and other bulbs and corms in pots in the house, but this is not so easy except for those who have greenhouses, and in that case I would advise them getting hold of a copy of *The A.B.C. of the Greenhouse. The A.B.C. of Bulbs and Corms*, goes into further details still and should be added to your collection without a doubt. Both the books are of course published by The English Universities Press.

CHAPTER 16

CACTI AND SUCCULENTS

I SPENT a very interesting time a year or two back with the Cactus growers of Bordighera. There is a large number of these specialised nurserymen there, and they sent literally thousands of these plants each season to Switzerland, France and various parts of Italy. Women on the Continent are far more Cactus-minded than we are, though it is true to say that the Cactus Societies founded since the war in this country are making great strides.

I always think of Cacti and Succulents as plants which grow under peculiar conditions. Few members of the Cactus family have leaves, but most of them have large or small spines. These spring in almost every case from a little cushion known as an areole. Look for the areoles, and, if they are present, you may almost certainly claim that the plant is a Cactus, whereas if no areoles are present, then it will go into the Succulent class.

Some of the plants grown as Cactus look like little stones in the ground, others I have seen in South Africa and in German South-West Africa (as it then was) grow very tall indeed and bear edible fruits. Some plants occasionally produce the most brilliant blooms, but few are spherical. Some are elongated like pencils; most of them are green; some of them resemble in colour the rocks among which they live.

Most people would not consider Cacti to be flowering plants, and yet you can have the most brilliant blooms when you grow the different species. I have seen orange, yellow, scarlet and pink flowers in profusion in Italy. Some of the Cacti flower at night time and these late nocturnal flowerers usually bear immense white blooms. They are ordinarily very sweetly-scented, but may only last a few hours. Some blooms on the other hand may be open for several days.

It is not always known that Cacti will bear fruits or berries. Sometimes it is true these are hidden in the wool-like substance which grows out of the side of the plant. The small flowers of the Mammillarias for instance are followed by masses of little scarlet berries. It is interesting to see the flowers of this season with the berries produced by last year's blossoms below. I was told just in Italy that it is possible to have a Mammillaria which bears fruits tasting something like strawberries. Some of the Echinocacti have edible berries also, and these may be almost as big as cherries.

One should grow indoors the Cacti and Succulents which are normally happy in the open desert and not try and cultivate the species which are found in the tropical forests. The desert kinds have to suffer long periods of drought. They grow in the most beautiful, clean, dry air. They are very occasionally watered by some tropical rain, but this soon drains away and so they have to store what they can. Some of the species have far-spreading surface roots, so that they may " suck in " the moisture whenever it should rain.

Try, therefore, to keep a Cactus indoors in a spot where it will get fresh air, lots of sunshine, and where it will be never over-watered or coddled. It is seldom that Cactus plants need feeding. Look at Chapter 3 and note the compost used. It must be open and the drainage perfect. More Cactus plants die of over-watering and feeding than from actual neglect. Don't, however, let the plants get frozen, but keep them away from windows in the winter.

Compost

Many shops and horticultural sundriesmen are willing to provide the right compost for Cacti. If there is a slight alteration to be made, then one can say that for the Phyllocacti one can use a little more peat than for the other types. Use clean pots, fill them up about one third of the way with broken crocks, and then put in the compost. Some people put over the crocks a few lumps of burnt clay. The roots should always be spread out in the soil and more of the compost is then put in position until the neck of the plant is covered. Half an inch of space is usually left between the surface of the soil and the rim of the pot, so that watering can be carried out as and when necessary.

Potting

Never pot firmly, just tap the container on the bench two or three times, and this will allow the compost to settle around the roots of the plants naturally. Those who are potting on plants with spines should wear gloves during the process. Incidentally, most of the re-potting or potting up is done during the early spring. Plants always grow better if they are given reasonable root room, and the converse is true. Thus if you restrict the roots the plants are dwarf. This is sometimes an advantage in a small house.

Where to grow

You can have the Cacti on the mantelpiece or on the windowsill, but the latter is undoubtedly the better position. The only danger here, as I have already said, is frost, and it pays to move the plants into the middle of the room at night-time in the winter. Give the plants plenty of room to develop; don't stand them too close together. Keep the windowpanes quite clean so that the Cacti can get as much sunlight as possible, and don't be afraid to open the windows in the summer, because the plants do like fresh air. It pays to keep the top of the window open night and day in fact, in warm weather.

If you live in a town, beware of fogs. These do a great deal of harm to Cacti and Succulents. Keep the windows shut tightly and, if fog should seriously get into a room, put a little ammonia in a saucer and stand this on the floor with the door shut for a few hours. A room heated and lit with electricity is much better for Cacti than a room with a gas fire. Even ordinary fires may be too hot for Cactus plants, though of course if they are on the windowsill they will be well away from the heat.

Watering

People sometimes ask me to give them rules about watering, and this is very difficult indeed to do. First of all it can be said that it is better to use rain water than water from a tap, and the modern system of chlorinating water in reservoirs is not at all helpful to the plants we are trying to grow. It helps if the water can be stood for 2 or 3 hours in the room or at least in full sunshine, before it is used for watering or spraying over.

Try and get the watering done very early in the morning before the plants get hot. If this is impossible, water them late in the afternoon. Only give water when absolutely necessary. The Cacti will not wilt when they need water, but on the other hand they certainly won't suffer if watering is postponed for three or four days. On the whole I give my Cacti water once a week in the winter and twice a week in the summer. The exceptions to the rule are the plants in the very tiny pots which have to stand on the window-ledge, and these may get a little drop of water every evening.

With the Echinopsis and Echinocacti, don't pour water over the plants, or else some of it may be retained in the top and cause rotting off to take place. It is never advisable, in fact, to pour water over any species of Cacti, but this doesn't mean to say that syringing shouldn't be done. A syringing helps in order to provide dew. It is best carried out very early in the morning, and it should be done on the days when one isn't going to water. Syringing is particularly important in the cases of plants grown in centrally-heated rooms.

Some plants need less water than others; for instance, in the case of the Opuntias, I seldom give them a drink more than once a month in the winter. The Mammillarias may be left for three weeks. They, for some reason or another, grow very happily in dry soil. In addition to watering, it is possible to scratch the surface of the soil with a little pointed label so as to allow the roots to get air. It also gives an opportunity for the water to get through quickly.

Temperatures

Most species of Cacti tolerate lower temperatures than

they normally have to put up with in their natural habitat. They don't want to be fussed over and they are certainly not difficult to grow. Though in Chapter 3, I have purposely given a general compost for Cacti, it is possible when one becomes an absolute Cactus fan to vary the soil mixture somewhat for the different species. Dr. J. Borg for instance, in his book *Cacti*, gives a list of some 16 different composts and tells which species will grow best in each. The beginner, however, will find that there is no need to vary from the standardised compost given.

SPECIES KNOWN AND GROWN

I believe that there are over 2,000 species known, and Dr. J. Borg devotes 377 pages to these! It is as well, however, to stick to the simple genera which are easy to grow in houses and flats.

Herewith you will find below the types, species and varieties which have been found to do well in houses and flats.

CEPHALOCEREUS

The plants of this genus normally grow in columns either singly or branched. Many of the plants have masses of hair or white wool at or near the top. The flowers appear at night and are small and hidden, the plants are small and round.

Species Cultivated:

C. senilis. Grows slowly, is covered with long soft wavy white hairs. Fruit violet-coloured. Can be raised easily from seed. Does well in sun, requires very little water.

C. palmeri. Is usually much branched, has whitish hair often 2 inches long. Flowers purplish as a rule. Fruits red.

CEREUS

(Torch Thistle)

There are some 26 species which are "tree-like". The flowers are funnel shaped. Likes warmth but not bright sunshine. Should never be allowed to dry out completely. When fruits appear they are usually edible.

Species Cultivated:

C. coerulescens. Grow like a little shrub or tree. Flowers are usually large and come out in the day, the petals are brown on the outside and white inside.

C. jamacuru (Syn. *C. validus*). A nice strong erect grower, stems often 6 inches in diameter. White flowers come out at night. The stems are often bluey in the first few years.

ECHINOCACTUS

Only a few species are now in this genus. Most have cylindrical stems. The flowers are yellow as a rule and almost hidden by wool. The fruits are white, scaly and woolly. Prefer a limy, gritty, medium rich soil. Give them plenty of water in the summer months. Shade from the strongest sun. In the winter give a minimum of water but lots of light.

Species Cultivated:

E. grusonii, often called the Golden Barrel or Golden Ball cactus. Produces curved golden spines. Flowers yellow inside, brown outside. Whole plant globular in shape.

E. ingens, usually purple towards the top, plus some " wool." Flowers yellow inside and red without. Grows globular or oblong in shape.

ECHINOCEREUS

The plants on the whole form clumps. The stems are short cylindrical and often bristly. The flowers open in the day time. Choose a medium, rich limy soil, plus full sun. Give plenty of water in the summer. The only fault is that the plants don't live as long as many other species.

Species cultivated:

E. chloranthus, quite cylindrical, covered with sharp spines. Flowers yellowish green which are borne on the sides of the stem.

E. dasycanthus A cylindrical type, which generally branches from the base. Has large flowers, funnel shaped, yellow. The spines start by being red and then turn grey.

E. delaitii. This is often erroniously called the Old Man Cactus, a name which truly belongs to Cephalocereus senilis, it is stiff stemmed and covered with long white hairs. Grows

10 inches high in the end and bears pink flowers on the sides of the stems.

ECHINOPSIS

(The Sea Urchin Cactus)

The plants are globular and have prominent ribs. The flowers are funnel shaped, the fruit that follows is fleshy and hairy. Give the plants plenty of water in the summer and lots of sun.

E. eyriessii (Syn. Echinocactus eyriesii). Has many horticultural forms such as shelkasei with dark brown " wool " and grandiflora with sharp ribs and dark pink flowers. Cylindrical on the whole stems often 6 inches across with 11–18 straight, sharp ribs. Flowers are white and are borne near the top.

E. multiplex (Syn. *Cereus multiplex*). Usually much branched with sweet smelling blooms. Stems 12 inches across. Flowers funnel-shaped, rose coloured. There is a cristate form.

EPIPHYLLUM

The branches are usually flattened and leaf-like. The flowers are so beautiful that the plants have been called " The Orchid Cactus ". The flowers bloom in the day-time. The fruits are usually edible and tasty. Give the plants full sun in the summer, or if you like, have them outside on the window sill. On the whole the kinds given below are easy to grow.

E. pittieri. Branches hang slightly. Flowers are hyacinth scented and night flowering.

N.B. The trade offer numerous hybrids such as Jean Dupois, Joseph de Laet, Purpur Koenig and Toleda, all of which are worth growing.

MAMMILARIA

(The Pin-cushion cactus)

A genus containing over 200 species. The plants are globular, low and have no ribs. It does however bear prominent warts, which may be woolly or hairy. The flowers are shaped like bells. The fruits are red and club shaped. The plants prefer full sun on the whole. Keep them cool and dry over the winter. They are on the whole lime lovers, so we usually put a little extra in the compost.

M. bocasana. A clustering and mound forming type. The stems are globular, bluish green in colour. The flowers are white with a red mid-rib. There is a cristate form also.

M. elegans. A very spiny type which starts by being solitary and then clusters and sprouts when older. Stems globular eventually 3 inches across. Flowers carmine red.

M. gracilis (Syn. *M. echinaria*). A branching and cluster-forming type which produces offsets which root easily. The stems are cylindrical and 2 inches thick. Looks like a " club " when growing.

M. schelhasei. A cluster-forming type. Globular growing 2 inches across. Flowers 1 inch long yellow or pinkish white with a red mid-rib.

M. wildii, included because it likes central-heated rooms. It must have a warm dry atmosphere during the winter. Grows cylindrical, often a bluish green shade. Flowers ½ an inch across white within and a red band without. There is a beautiful cristate form.

OPUNTIA

A genus with over 300 species nearly all of which have flattened, fleshy, green stems. Many opuntias are called the Indian Fig or the Fig-cactus. Handle all plants carefully because the tips of the spines attach themselves quickly to the skin and cause irritation. Grow them in full sun and give them dry conditions in the winter.

Species Cultivated:

O. bergeriana. Grows like a tree and eventually the trunk may be 16 inches across! The spines are yellowish, the flowers dark red with pink stamens.

O. leucotricha. Also tree-like with many branches, the joints are usually elliptical and they are covered with white bristles. The flowers are yellow and have a red centre to them.

O. ranesquei (Syn. *O. humifusa*). A spreading prostrate type. It roots readily from the lower edge of the joints. The joints are egg-shaped often 5 inches long and 4 inches wide. The flowers are yellow and large.

Oerinacea var. *ursina,* known as the Grizzly Bear cactus, comes from the Californian desert. Small jointed, hair-like spines. Flowers yellow to pink.

PHYLLOCACTUS

This species is usually found today under Epiphyllum.

ZYGOCACTUS

This is the Christmas Cactus, so called because it often blooms at Christmas time. It flowers any time from late October to January. Keep in a warm and shady place during the summer. Keep fairly moist from February onwards. Spray over with scent-spray filled with water in the summer.

Species Cultivated:

Z. truncatus. A bushy much branched type with fuchsia-like flowers of a deep red colour. Fruits dull red. Has been called the Crab cactus.

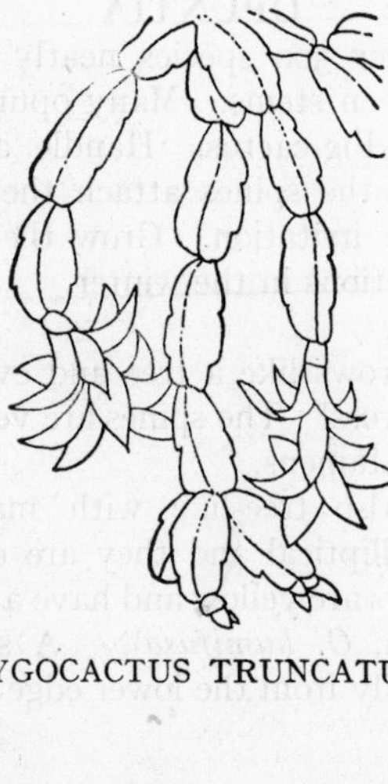

THE CHRISTMAS CACTUS.

ZYGOCACTUS TRUNCATUS.

THE SUCCULENTS

In addition to the Cacti there are considerable quantities of species of succulent plants listed, by the various authorities. Only a few species and varieties are known to do well under indoor conditions and it is on these that the book concentrates.

Cultivation in nearly all respects is the same for succulents as that described for Cacti and any special requirements will be noted against individual species or varieties.

Temperatures

A number of commonly-grown succulents can support a slightly lower winter temperature than the Cacti and the pots should never be allowed to dry out completely. Frost is, of course, fatal.

Watering

During the resting period, it is important to water much more sparingly than other times. The time of the year for undergoing this dormant or resting period will vary from species to species, but can often be recognised by a slight shrivelling of the plant, which does not mean that it is dying. It is better to under-water than over-water!

Propagation

This is very easy with some succulent plants, e.g., with those which produce suckers that can be potted-up. Others have cuttings which strike readily without heat.

There are a number, however, which are difficult to raise either from seed or cuttings in the home.

AICHRYSON

Producing rosettes of leaves. This is a very hardy plant and can go outside in the summer. It likes light, but not full sunlight. Water moderately, but do not over-water. Can be propagated by its leaf rosettes, which will strike easily.

Species cultivated:

A. domesticum (Syn. *Sempervivum tortuosum*).

AGAVE

Has stiff, spiny leaves in rosettes. Does not usually flower in the house.

Propagation:

Generally by suckers produced around old plants.

They are sun-lovers and grow to a big size. Can go out in the summer and can be fairly cool in the winter.

Feed a little with weak liquid manure in the summer.

Species cultivated:

A. *filifera* is a small plant with greyish-green leaves and white fibres hanging from them.

A. *stricta* is the Hedgehog Agave. It is trunkless and has pale or purplish leaves.

A. *Victoriae reginae* has dark-green leaves with grey margins.

A. *Americana variegata*—the variegated kind.

ALOE

Very similar to the Agave, but the flowering stalk is produced at the side of the rosette.

Prefers to be in the light and can go out in the garden in the summer.

Keep cool in winter months.

Species cultivated:

A. *arborescens* has long, toothed foliage. Reproduction by side shoots.

A. *variegata* has thick, dark-green leaves with white bands, Reproduction by suckers.

CRASSULA

Has round, fleshy leaves and star-shaped flowers.

Do not grow in full sunlight.

Propagation:

By cuttings, which root easily.

Species cultivated:

C. *argentea* (Syn. C. *portulacea*). Has thick, green and shining leaves. Rarely flowers in the house.

C. *falcata* (Syn. *Rochea falcata*). Has bright red flowers in August.

C. pyramidalis has dark green leaves, which are tightly packed and seem to form a little four-sided column.

ECHEVERIA

Has broad leaves in rosettes. The flowers are often bell-shaped.

Propagation:

By cuttings.

Watering:

Should only be watered when nearly dust-dry. Warm conditions in summer and moderate in winter.

Not one of the easiest.

Species cultivated:

E. amoena has greyish-coloured leaves tinted with red, which are born in tiny rosettes.

E. retusa hybrids are commonly grown and have grey-green leaves in rosettes with reddish tints. The bright red flowers are produced on tall stems in January.

EUPHORBIA

Most have insignificant flowers and stems resembling columns. Some have spikes and many have no leaves. Most Euphorbias discharge a milky juice when cut. This juice may cause dermatitis on some people.

Propagation:

By stem cuttings and is not easy in the home.

Light:

Must have lots of light and warm conditions throughout the winter.

Keep dryish.

Species cultivated:

E. acrurensis has tree-like stems and spines which are long and grey with dark tips.

E. submammillaris has many spiny branches with toothed ridges. The bracts are purple and tiny.

E. splendens, bright red bracts, "Crown of Thorns."

GASTERIA

Has thick leaves crowded with rosettes. The flowers are red or rose in racemes.

Propagation:

By suckers.

Watering:

Keep dryish in winter.

This is an easy plant to grow.

Species cultivated:

There is a number of hybrids and varieties in cultivation.

KALANCHOE

Has scarlet flowers and fleshy leaves.

Propagation:

By stem or leaf cuttings, or by seeds.

They like the sun and warmth during the winter. Keep in small pots.

Watering:

Only water when pots have practically dried out.

Species cultivated:

K. Blossfeldiana is commonly cultivated.

KLEINIA

A small easily-grown succulent plant from Africa.

Propagation:

By cuttings and runners.

Watering:

Keep very dry at all seasons.

Species cultivated:

K. repens (Syn. *Senecio succulentus. Cocalia repens*). Has stems which are almost cylindrical and pale yellow flowers.

MESEMBRYANTHEMUM

A very well-known group of Succulents. Certain species have now been segregated into different genera.

The cultivation of the various indoor species is more or less the same.

Propagation:

Very easy by cuttings, most of which can be struck in the home.

Watering:

Not done unless absolutely necessary.

Species cultivated:

A number of plants of the following genera and species are commonly cultivated and make useful house plants:

Conophytum (Cone-Plant). Most of the plants of this genus look like little brown or green pebbles when they are not in flower.

Didymaotus. The plants usually appear like little inverted boats, with a V-slice cut in the centre.

Lithops. The plants are again like stones.

Aptenia cordifolia (Syn. *Mesembryanthemum cordifolium*) has leaves like little, grey-green chipped potatoes and is a very common house plant.

SEMPERVIVUM

(Houseleek)

These little plants with rosettes of leaves are very hardy.

Propagation:

By rooting the young rosettes.

Species cultivated:

S. tectorum is the Common or Roof Houseleek.

There are numerous other varieties.

They can tolerate most indoor conditions.

S. arachnoideum (the Spider Houseleek), very pretty.

INDEX